What people are saying about

Jim McKenzie and *One Generation to the Next*

"I don't know what I was expecting when I opened *One Generation to the Next*. But I certainly was not expecting to be touched, challenged, and inspired the way this book does. This book isn't just for the next generation: it's for me. I don't know that I've ever encountered so much kindness, faithfulness, and clarity condensed into one slender work. I'm glad Jim McKenzie is in the world, and I'm glad his words here are, too."

KAREN SWALLOW PRIOR, author of *The Evangelical Imagination: How Stories, Images, and Metaphors Created a Culture in Crisis*

"As parents, what greater prayer do we have for our children than to know and follow Jesus? In a time in history in which we do not prioritize cross-generational relationships as we should, this book is a gem. In a way that only an educator, parent, and follower of Jesus could, Jim distills the foundations of a life with Christ into a text that is Biblically sound, approachable, moving, and transformative all at once."

DR. KATIE WIENS, Executive Director, Council on Educational Standards and Accountability

"In *One Generation to the Next,* Jim McKenzie shares a vision for faithful devotion to Jesus, free from the cultural and political entanglements common today. Drawing from his own life experience, Jim combines stories and Scripture to offer the next generation sound wisdom and guidance for their own faith journey. And while he has written to teens and young adults, readers of all ages will find encouragement in his words. *One Generation to the Next* is a welcomed guide for all who want to follow Jesus."

DAVID EATON, CEO of Axis and author of
Smartphone Sanity and *Engaging Your Teen's World*

"Like apples of gold in settings of silver, this book serves up a timely offering of Christian thought for prudent living and human flourishing. In a generation of digital natives, young adults are experiencing information overload, often leading to a gap in their ability to filter what is biblically true from what is socially acceptable. This disconnect between their faith journey and cultural trends, impacts their identity in ways that could be more deforming than transforming. In *One Generation to The Next,* Jim McKenzie is a voice of discipleship, sharing pathways for young adults to "not conform to this world but be transformed by the renewing of [their] mind," setting their lived experiences and future hopes on Jesus Christ alone."

STEVENER GASKIN, JR., Director of Intercultural Arts & Media |
Student Engagement, Wheaton College

"In a world where social media and pop culture are trying to raise our kids, I'm so thankful for voices like Jim McKenzie's. He speaks with the wisdom and compassion of someone who's spent his life pouring into young people, all the while educating and empowering them to live out the teachings of Jesus with boldness. This book is a field manual for a generation that's searching for their way and will only find it in Him."

HAVILAH CUNNINGTON,
Founder of *Truth to Table*

"*One Generation to the Next* is a book that should be read over and over again. Grounded in biblical wisdom, this invaluable resource will offer anyone raising children or working with students the hope necessary to pass on the infinite truths of God's Word and love. Jim writes with a humility that will draw you in and inspire you to rightly focus your life on passing along the most important things in this life…that which is linked to the next. The need to pass on what truly matters to the next generation may never be greater than it is right now, and this book will guide you on the path to effectively doing so for God's glory. Read it. Highlight it. Mark in it. And, then do it again. This book may just change your life like it did Jim's."

MATT THOMAS, Ed.D., Executive Director,
Baylor's Center for School Leadership

"Part of why I love this book is because we get much of Jim's honest, hilarious, inspiring life--Jim the lifeguard, Jim the midnight football player, Jim the Samaritan, Jim the snake-charmer. But at the heart of it is dad-Jim and teacher-Jim, inviting the next generation to join him in following Jesus as the way the truth and the life—in all its fullness. In so doing, Jim gently but courageously cuts through a number of false narratives that creep into our assumptions about what that Jesus-way actually means. I'm a part of Jim's generation. But I want to join Jim in reading the Bible as our improv script for following Jesus too. And this book has helped me to do exactly that."

JUSTIN COOK, Director of Learning,
Edvance Christian Schools Association

"Judges 2:10 says, "After that whole generation had been gathered to their ancestors, another generation grew up who knew neither the Lord nor what he had done for Israel." How sobering and saddening that the fear and knowledge of God died but one generation after He fulfilled His promise to Israel. And in many ways, we find ourselves similarly situated today; a generation that knows less of God than their parents. But, into this void of understanding comes *One Generation to the Next*, a book that seeks to reverse the pattern so that this generation will become the seedbed for stronger faith in the next. It is a must read for every parent and child!"

NONA JONES, Author of *Killing Comparison*,
and Tech Executive

"Imparting biblical wisdom to our children is a daunting task. Jim McKenzie's *One Generation to the Next* is a giant leap in the right direction. With his conversational style and engaging personal stories, McKenzie throws his own humanity into every page, engaging the reader at the emotional, academic, and spiritual levels."

MICHAEL BURROUGHS, Executive Director,
League of Christian Schools

"This is a discipleship book that taught me plenty about what I already know. Jim weaves his own story with insightful biblical teaching that gently corrects and inspires us to better follow Jesus. There are things to *stir up* the reader, but Jim's life and stories with their humility and sincerity provided a credible voice that helped me to *listen slowly* rather than to dismiss."

BISHOP RON KUYKENDALL, Ph.D, Executive Chaplain to the
National Director & Chaplain to the Board for the
International Order of St. Luke the Physician

"If in the future you run into author Jim McKenzie and he has a fresh tattoo on his forehead reading "Make Allowances" he will probably recommend that you read this book to discover the story behind it. Beyond that insight, you will also read a book full of personal anecdotes, scriptural reflections, with meaningful connections drawn between the two. In this book, Jim provides fresh perspectives on familiar concepts, encouraging the reader to 'see anew.'"

GAYLE MONSMA, Executive Director at
The Prairie Centre for Christian Education

"Judges 2:10 mentions a time in the history of Israel when "there arose another generation after them who did not know the Lord...." That verse serves as a reminder that we have not been successful as Christian leaders, educators, and parents if we only cultivate the faith in our generation and do not pass on the faith to the generation coming behind us. Jim McKenzie has given us a helpful resource in empowering the next generation with a faith that can sustain them. Jim carefully weaves personal stories, and the stories of others, into the principles and practices he offers in this book. He stays in close proximity to the Scriptures and directs our attention to the mission of Jesus to love the world God loves in a way that promotes peace and justice. *One Generation to the Next* is a call to lead an action-oriented life as we follow Jesus in the ways of God's goodness. The practices in this book will anchor all of us in the faith like a fixed rope in an underwater cave."

DEREK VREELAND, pastor and author of *Centering Jesus*

"I love this book! Jim says he wrote *One Generation to the Next* to guide young Christians in their personal faith journeys. But this book is for all of us. Each of his chapters and subchapters can stand on its own as an inspiring meditation. Jim is a gifted writer who skillfully weaves together personal, real-life stories with applications from the Bible and leading scholars. The result is an extremely readable, joyful reflection on what it means to be a Christian in our complex times."

DR. DAVID HAHN, Executive Director,
Association of Lutheran Secondary Schools

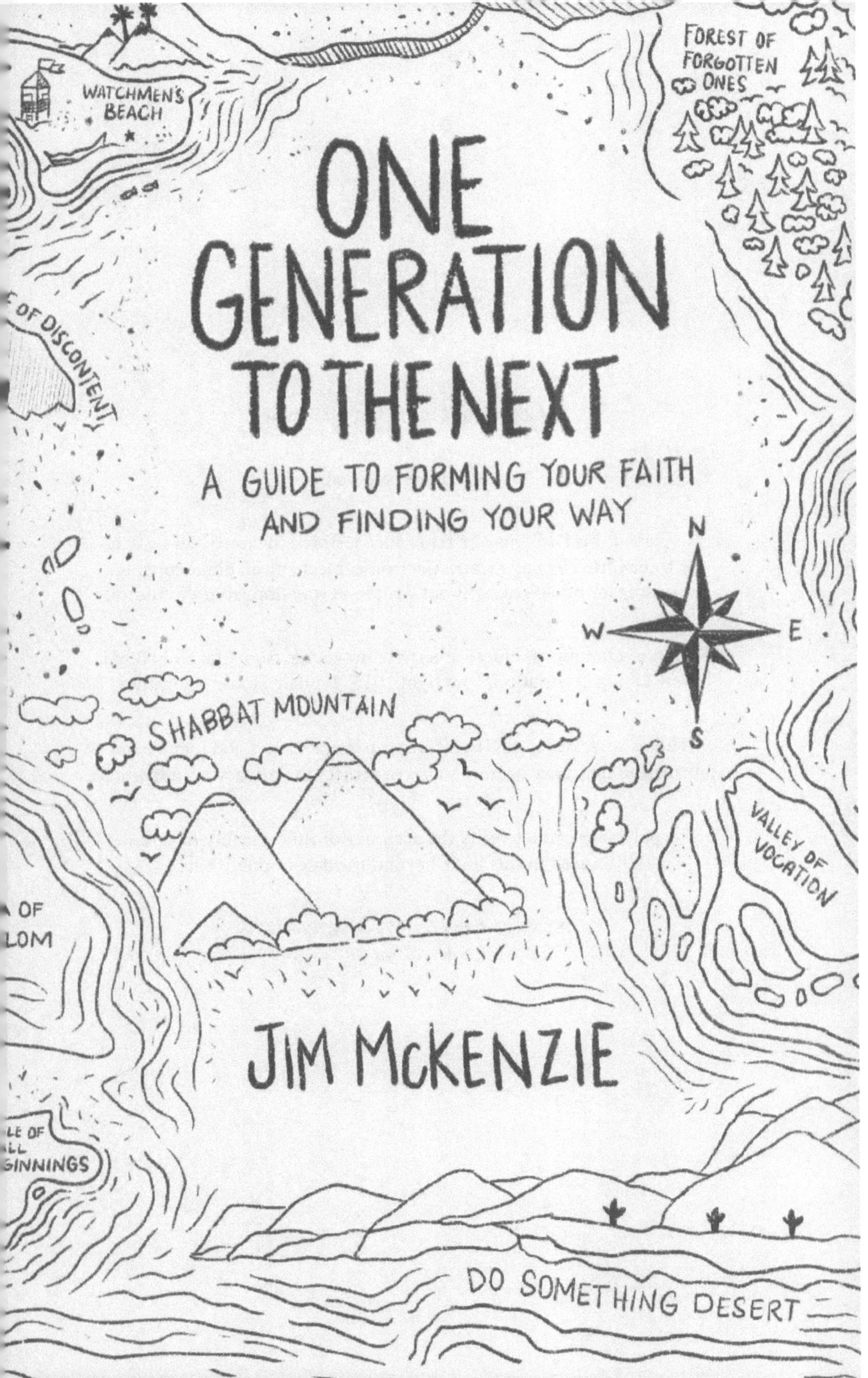

WATCHMEN'S BEACH
FOREST OF FORGOTTEN ONES
OF DISCONTENT
ONE GENERATION TO THE NEXT
A GUIDE TO FORMING YOUR FAITH AND FINDING YOUR WAY
N
W   E
S
SHABBAT MOUNTAIN
VALLEY OF VOCATION
OF LOM
JIM MCKENZIE
LE OF LL GINNINGS
DO SOMETHING DESERT

For Colby, Casey, Cooper, Carter, and Darcy:
May you set your hope anew on God
and tell of His wondrous works to a new generation.

Table of Contents

O my people, listen to my instructions.
Open your ears to what I am saying,
for I will speak to you in a parable.
I will teach you hidden lessons from our past—
stories we have heard and known,
stories our ancestors handed down to us.
We will not hide these truths from our children;
we will tell the next generation
about the glorious deeds of the Lord,
about his power and his mighty wonders.
For he issued his laws to Jacob;
he gave his instructions to Israel.
He commanded our ancestors
to teach them to their children,
so the next generation might know them—
even the children not yet born—
and they in turn will teach their own children.
So each generation should set its hope anew on God,
not forgetting his glorious miracles
and obeying his commands.
—Psalm 78:1-7—

Foreword

Starting in sixth grade, every year we vowed that we were only putting our youngest daughter at The Rock School for that year and that next year we'd find another school.

She'd finished fifth grade at a tiny, hybrid homeschool setting and after a reasonably extensive search, we decided on The Rock School as the full-time destination for her for sixth grade year. TRS was faith-based and a little larger than where she'd been. Plus, they said the right things about valuing the children's education.

I try not to worship at the idol of educational credentials, but holding degrees from Duke and Harvard Law, I view those experiences as critical to my personal development, and don't want to see either of our daughters' educations get shortchanged. At the same time, our Christian faith is paramount for us, and we didn't want to sacrifice the quest for Truth at the altar of Information.

"It'll be a soft landing spot for her," we told ourselves about sixth grade at TRS. "Once she's had a year to acclimate to a full-time setting, we'll find another option." After all, we live in a university town with some excellent educational opportunities.

Then she started school and we met Jim McKenzie, Headmaster of TRS.

Still, each Spring we'd tell ourselves that it was just for a year, that we'd figure out the perfect long-term solution for the following year.

"We'll probably move her in a year," my wife and I agreed. Even after that first year, and each subsequent one, during which she had a good experience, we'd say the same thing.

We were like the Dread Pirate Roberts in one of our family's favorite movies, *The Princess Bride*.

"Good night, Westley. Good work. Sleep well. I'll most likely kill you in the morning," the pirate told Westley every night before bed.

"Okay, Ellie. Another year at TRS. We're sure it'll go well. And then next year we'll find the perfect school for you," we'd tell her every Spring when we'd send in her re-enrollment forms.

Like Westley, she came to believe it less and less over time.

We made one more concerted push before Ellie began high school, touring campuses and attending information sessions. After all the tours, meetings, and sessions…we ended up at TRS.

Why?

Leadership and heart.

Actually, leadership *with* heart.

Jim was always thoughtful, disciplined and deliberate. I watched him navigate a number of situations throughout our daughter's seven years at TRS that underscored my faith in his leadership abilities.

But while I'd love for him to share on his approach to leadership, this book is about something even more important which served as the foundation for his leadership: Christian formation.

Our daughter was confronted with Jim's genuine concern for her heart every Monday when he spoke at Chapel as well as other informal times throughout the week.

Everything went through his filter of how our faith should inform our lives. In curriculum decisions, student behavior (and misbehavior), down to whether and when to mask during Covid or whether to reopen the school at all, the question was asked how Christ's sacrificial model should guide us.

Our feelings, our rights, our wishes…all these are important. But as followers of Jesus who are to be salt and light in the world, those can't be the end of our inquiry. And so it wasn't at The Rock School.

Jim made sure they were wrestling with the right questions in the right ways and how they should view themselves in light of the larger world. Seeing themselves as important, but that others were just as important.
True humility in Christ.

We'd reopen the "debate" every year as to whether it was the best setting for Ellie, but the question was merely *pro forma* by the middle of her high school career. Even if the school hadn't maintained the focus on educational innovation, even if another school had a sure-fire formula to access the Ivy League, Jim's focus on forming their hearts made the difference.

My generation matters. How I live out my faith matters. A lot.
Especially to help the next generation along.

I was blessed to watch Jim McKenzie focus on that next generation for seven years. Now, in the pages to follow, you'll have the opportunity to see his approach for yourself and be moved, inspired and transformed. And the chance that you won't be blessed as I have been is simply
Inconceivable.

Nathan Whitaker
Gainesville, FL
#1 New York Times bestselling author

Introduction

As I write this book, my oldest son is entering his senior year of high school at the Christian school where I serve as the headmaster. At the end of this year, he will walk across the graduation stage, where I will shake his hand and give him his diploma. We will momentarily pose for the event photographer, and then he will continue across the stage and back to his seat. After a few more minutes, he will stand to face the audience, turn his tassel, and launch his cap into the air as I pronounce that he and his peers are officially high school graduates.

Outwardly, I will rejoice in my son's accomplishments and the bright future that's ahead of him. Inwardly, I will mourn, reconciling my loss as this season of life comes to an end.

Since he was born, I have always tried my best as his father to offer him love, encouragement, and direction. To make sure he was ready for this day. But, in truth, I wonder, did I do enough? Did I do it right? Few things require more faith in life than that which is required for a parent to let a child go. Even now, as I write those words, I feel a tinge of anxiety nipping at my soul. I can trust God with my own life, but truthfully, it feels harder to do that with my son's life.

From this moment on, the decisions he will make will almost entirely be his own. His college major. His career path. His marriage plans. His decision to follow Jesus. But because he is wise, he will seek counsel along the way.

So, this book is written to be a guide for him. And for my younger sons and daughter who will also one day grow up and leave home. And for all the other students who have turned their tassels at the graduations I have presided over for twenty years. It's for all the children, teens, and young adults that I've crossed paths with over the last thirty years. And it's for all those I've yet to meet. This book is for you.

In your hero's journey, I hope that I can be a trusted guide.

This book is my attempt to share the lessons I've learned about the Christian faith. But I'm not a theologian. I didn't go to seminary. I don't pastor a church. I'm an educator. I love to teach. This book represents my lesson plans if I were to teach a class entitled, "Following Jesus." My deep hope is that this book encourages you in your own pursuit of Him.

Small Beginnings

God's people have been taken captive. Their city has been destroyed. They were forced to travel hundreds of miles to live in a foreign land under the rule of the Babylonian empire. After seventy years, God delivers them from their oppressors, and they are finally able to return to Jerusalem.

But now they've got the monumental task of rebuilding both their lives and the temple. There are no construction crews to hire, no cranes, and no concrete trucks. There is no Home Depot in town where they can go purchase supplies. This project is going to take eighteen years to complete.

But as they are just getting started, God offers this encouragement: "Do not despise these small beginnings, for the Lord rejoices to see the work begin, to see the plumb line in Zerubbabel's hand."[1] God did not hold his delight until the temple was finished eighteen years later, but rather delighted to see the work begin. The moment Zerubbabel picked up the first tool to get started, God smiled.

In whatever season you find yourself at this moment, God delights to see you begin. He's not waiting for you to graduate high school or complete your college degree. He's not waiting until you start a career or launch a new business. He's not waiting for you to find a spouse or birth a child. The moment you write your name on the exam paper or ask that girl out on a first date, God is already delighting in you to see the work begin.

God knew the temple would be built. But He was most excited to see the work get started. In this same way, God already knows the good work that you will accomplish in this lifetime, but He rejoices to see you begin, no matter how small or inconsequential that beginning may seem.

You may be a person of great faith or little faith or no faith at all. But as you begin this journey to build the temple of your Christian faith and explore what it means to follow Jesus in your world, be encouraged, knowing that the Lord rejoices to see this work begin in you.

Each chapter of this book presents a singular idea—a principle or practice—that has served me well in my journey with Jesus. I offer them to you as a guide. I don't know what the future holds, but I know the One who holds the future and I invite you to orient your life around Him. May these pages be a compass that points you to Jesus, our north star.

He is already smiling upon you. Let the journey begin.

---

[1] Zechariah 4:10

CHAPTER ONE

Seek Shalom

Imagine spending fourteen months putting together a 6000-piece jigsaw puzzle only to discover there is still one missing piece.

During the three months that the entire country was basically shut down during the pandemic, our family passed the time by doing jigsaw puzzles together. We'd set up a small card table in our living room so we could keep the puzzle out and work at it whenever inspiration would strike. Usually, one of us would stop and add a few pieces and, before long, other members of our family would jump in and help. We'd work at it for a while, usually taking a break whenever we hit a wall and couldn't place a new piece after a few minutes. The puzzle would sit there for some time until someone decided to take another run at it, and then we'd all be back around the card table for another go.

We started simple. First, we completed a 200-piece NASA puzzle of the planet Mars (it was a round puzzle, not square, so that was fun.) Next, we upgraded to a 500-piece landscape puzzle of a beautiful photo of a national park. That one took a few weeks to finish, but once it was done, no one wanted to break it apart. There was this enormous sense of accomplishment in completing the puzzle, so we kept it intact but moved it to an empty shelf in another room so we could start a new puzzle on the designated card table. Given our recent successes, and feeling rather ambitious this time, we bought a 1000-piece puzzle for our next challenge. It featured a photo of hundreds of little Hershey chocolate candies poured out on a table. When we opened the box and dumped the contents onto our puzzle table, we discovered what can only be described as a thousand tiny, identical brown cardboard pieces.

Although a bit discouraged by the seemingly difficult task before us, we immediately chose to step up to the challenge. We gave ourselves a little pep talk, and then we attacked that puzzle with a fervor and dedication to finish what we were starting. But that commitment quickly began to wane as the hours passed with little visible progress. After more than a week, we had yet to even complete the puzzle's rectangular border. A few weeks later, with barely the border complete and 900 loose pieces still floating on the table, the intervals between attempts at the puzzle by a family member were getting longer and longer. After more than a month without any noticeable evidence of progress, it became clear that this puzzle had defeated our family and that our threshold for puzzle pieces was probably going to remain at 500 or fewer. With a sad resentment, we brushed all the broken pieces back into the box and retired it to the top shelf in the back of some closet in the house, where it will wait to be sold at a neighborhood yard sale.

Hershey puzzle – 1, McKenzie family – 0.

Given our sad history with large puzzles, imagine my delight in reading a story about a man who spent fourteen months putting together a massive 6000-piece landscape puzzle. I saw a picture of the puzzle, and it is magnificent. It featured a glorious castle set up on a hill with a blue lake behind it and a mountain range set in the distance. I have such respect for the time and dedication it must have taken over the course of fourteen long months to complete this puzzle. The number of pieces that failed to go together when he tried to connect them. The frustration when piece after piece wouldn't fit and the elation when finally joining two together.

Imagine getting to the end, placing that final piece of the puzzle, and stepping back to admire your handiwork. And then, and only then, discovering there's a hole in the middle of the puzzle. You're one piece short. That's what happened to Robert Miles. Despite searching for it everywhere – the floor, the lid, under the puzzle itself – the missing piece was nowhere to be found. A 6000-piece puzzle that only has 5999 pieces.[2] How frustrating!

I know how my fellow puzzle completer must have felt. There are no more pieces, but it's not done. It's incomplete. It's unfinished. There's a hole right there in the middle of the whole darn thing!

We're empathetic to this story of the man and his missing puzzle piece because deep inside of each of us is a shared desire for things to be complete. To be whole. We can't stand the idea that the puzzle doesn't have its last piece. There's a satisfaction, a feeling that all is right, when we place the last piece to complete the puzzle. But until then, the puzzle gnaws at us in all its unfinishedness. It's not right until it's whole.

The Bible has a word that describes this same desire for our humanity. It's the Hebrew word *shalom*. We typically translate this word as peace. But I've come to understand that *shalom* has a much richer meaning.[3]

The word *shalom* appears in the Old Testament in a few different forms. As *shalom*, a noun, to describe peace or wholeness. It is used as *shalem*, a verb that means to make right or restore. We also see it as *shelem*, a peace offering, and as *shalem*, an adjective

---

[2] Adam Proskiw, "Kelowna man spent 14 months assembling massive jigsaw puzzle to find one missing piece," InfoNews online, December 6, 2017, https://infotel.ca/newsitem/kelowna-man-spent-14-months-assembling-massive-jigsaw-puzzle-to-find-one-missing-piece/it48317.

[3] I first encountered the concept of shalom as flourishing while listening to a presentation by Dan Beerens on "Student Flourishing in Christian Schools." I am grateful for his work and his friendship.

meaning loyal or devoted. In the New Testament, it's translated as *eirene*, the Greek noun we read as peace.

But theologian Nicholas Wolterstorff argues that translating *shalom* as "peace" has too many limitations.[4] Based on the historical and theological context, Wolterstorff believes that a better definition of *shalom* would be the word *flourishing*.

In his book, *Engaging God's World*, Neal Plantinga defines shalom as "the webbing together of God, humans, and all creation, in justice, fulfillment, and delight."

Tim Keller, writing in *Generous Justice*, states that "shalom means complete reconciliation, a state of the fullest flourishing in every dimension – physical, emotional, social, and spiritual – because all relationships are right, perfect, and filled with joy."

A simple definition that encompasses these two ideas and that of Wolterstorff's flourishing is to say that shalom is being rightly related to God, creation, others, and self, and finding joy in it.

Shalom, therefore, is a four-piece puzzle.

When our lives are rightly related to God, creation, others, and self, we find the kind of wholeness that we desire.

To find peace with God, with creation, with others, and with self is to find shalom.

Shalom, we could say, is a four-*peace* puzzle.

So, what does it look like to seek shalom? What does it mean to find peace with God? Let's turn to the Laodiceans for some guidance.

---

[4] "Nicolas Wolterstorff: It's Tied Together by Shalom," Faith & Leadership online, March 1, 2010, https://faithandleadership.com/nicholas-wolterstorff-its-tied-together-shalom.

Shalom With God

Have you ever been so disgusted by something you drank that you spit it out of your mouth? I was doing an Amazon search one day for sodas and I discovered some unusual drinks for sale in the United States:

- Bacon Soda
- Ranch Dressing Soda
- Grass Soda
- Pink Pepsi (strawberry & milk flavored)
- Onion Coke

Would you be willing to try any of these? While I'll admit that these drinks sound terrible, I don't think I would immediately spit them out. I just probably wouldn't take a second sip.

But sometimes, something is so disgusting that we spit it out of our mouths, even if it's not the best display of good manners at that moment. An almost involuntary reaction sweeps over us and we spew it out. We can't help ourselves.

Jesus says that this is his response to the church at Laodicea. The church must have left a bad taste in Jesus' mouth if he is willing to spit them out.

John of Patmos had a vision in which he was taken to heaven, and in the book of Revelation, he records all that he sees. In the opening chapters, Jesus tells John to write letters to seven churches, and in Chapter 3, he specifically addresses the church in Laodicea with these words:

"Write this letter to the angel of the church in Laodicea. This is the message from the one who is the Amen—the faithful and true witness, the beginning of God's new creation:

"I know all the things you do, that you are neither hot nor cold. I wish that you were one or the other! But since you are like lukewarm water, neither hot nor cold, I will spit you out of my mouth! You say, 'I am rich. I have everything I want. I don't need a thing!' And you don't realize that you are wretched and miserable and poor and blind and naked. So I advise you to buy gold from me—gold that has been purified by fire. Then you will be rich. Also buy white garments from me so you will not be shamed by your nakedness, and ointment for your eyes so you will be able to see. I correct and discipline everyone I love. So be diligent and turn from your indifference.

"Look! I stand at the door and knock. If you hear my voice and open the door, I will come in, and we will share a meal together as friends."

I grew up believing that this biblical text about hot and cold was a metaphor for our spiritual temperature. That to be "hot" meant to be "on fire" and passionate for God, and to be "cold" meant to be "cold-hearted" and far from God. To be "lukewarm" meant to be "meh" and sort of indifferent in my relationship with God. I was taught that Jesus' central message here – "I wish that you were either hot or cold" – was that it would be better for humans to either be "on fire" for God or be an atheist – "cold and distant" – than to be a lukewarm Christian that was a middle-of-the-road believer.

But what if that's not what Jesus meant? What if it wasn't a metaphor about our spiritual temperature and was, in fact, a geographical allusion rooted in the historical context of Laodicea?[5]

---

[5] Zach Hoag, "What Lukewarm in Laodicea Really Means," Bible Gateway Blog, June 28, 2017, https://www.biblegateway.com/blog/2017/06/what-lukewarm-in-laodicea-really-means/.

Laodicea was in an area of Asia Minor in what is now modern-day Turkey. It was situated between two other cities – Hierapolis to the north and Colossae to the south.

Hierapolis was known for its hot springs, and some even believed the waters had healing powers.

Colossae was home to cold springs, and people traveled there to enjoy their cool and refreshing waters.

But Laodicea had neither hot springs nor cold springs. Their water supply was provided from Colossae by an aqueduct system. This was thousands of years ago, so they didn't have the conveniences of modern plumbing. They didn't have air-tight, water-tight pipes, filtration systems, cooling systems, and sanitized storage tanks to manage their city's water supply. So as the water traveled the six-mile journey from Colossae to Laodicea along the open stone aqueduct system, the water would become warm and often undrinkable because of the contaminants it would acquire along the way.

When Jesus said to the Laodiceans that you are neither hot nor cold, it was in reference to the healing waters of the north and the refreshing waters of the south. Both were good, both were profitable. When Jesus called the Laodiceans lukewarm, he was comparing their faith to the tepid and undrinkable water of their city that residents would often spit from their mouths because of how disgusting it was to their lips.

Jesus chastised them for a Christianity that was as offensive as their water supply.

Why? The answer is found in verse 17:

"You say, 'I am rich. I have everything I want. I don't need a thing!' And you don't realize that you are wretched and miserable and poor and blind and naked."

Their self-reliance left a bad taste in Jesus' mouth.

We live in a culture in which self-reliance is applauded. We admire the self-made man and woman. We celebrate the stories of those who pull themselves up by their bootstraps. We cheer for those who set out to make it on their own, who turn down a helping hand, who determine to be the captains of their own ships. In short, we're a self-reliant people and proud of it.

But Jesus says our self-reliance makes us like the lukewarm water. Despite what we may want to believe, according to Jesus, self-reliance doesn't make us strong, it makes us sick.

Our self-reliance robs us of our self-reflection. Jesus criticized the Laodicean church, noting that because of their self-reliance – because of their belief that they "don't need a thing!" – they didn't even realize their true state, "wretched and miserable and poor and blind and naked."

What does it look like to seek shalom with God? It means abandoning our self-reliance and putting our full and complete trust in Jesus.

Jesus plus nothing equals everything.[6]
But, like Laodicea, we want to add to the equation.
Jesus plus my significant other equals everything.
Jesus plus my career goals equals everything.
Jesus plus athletic success equals everything.
Jesus plus my social status equals everything.
Jesus plus making money equals everything.
Jesus plus _______________ equals everything.
How do you fill in the blank?

When we rely solely on ourselves, we fail to realize our true condition as wretched and poor and naked and blind. But this is Jesus' promise to the Laodiceans and to us, if we'll commit ourselves fully to Him:

---

[6] Havilah Cunnington introduced this equation to our student ministry nearly twenty years ago and I never forgot it.

"So I advise you to buy gold from me—gold that has been purified by fire. Then you will be rich. Also buy white garments from me so you will not be shamed by your nakedness, and ointment for your eyes so you will be able to see."

God will provide for us. He will cover our shame. He will give us a clear vision of ourselves and our world.

Shalom is a four-peace puzzle.

Jesus plus nothing equals everything.

Surrender your self-reliance and allow the Lord to be your source and your guide.

Take hold of the first peace.

Shalom With Creation

The second piece of the shalom puzzle is creation.

As the Headmaster of a Christian school, I am the primary speaker in our Monday morning Chapel service for our K-12 students. I have this game I do sometimes with the students that I call "Preschool or Professional?" It's a contest where students must decide if what they are seeing or hearing was created by a preschool student or a professional.

One time I hosted "Preschool or Professional: Art Edition" in which I showed students a work of art, and they had to determine if it was created by a preschool student or a professional artist. I showed them ten different works of art, and they got every single answer right. (I didn't say it was a hard game, did I?). Our students had no trouble differentiating between preschool and Picasso. As we looked at some of the most famous paintings in history, it was not difficult to recognize the creative talent that captured the scene on canvas.

King David declared in Psalm 19:1-4,

"The heavens proclaim the glory of God.
The skies display his craftsmanship.
Day after day they continue to speak;
night after night they make him known.
They speak without a sound or word;
their voice is never heard.
Yet their message has gone throughout the earth,
and their words to all the world."

When we spend time in God's good creation, we see His hand-iwork. In the created world, we read His story, written "without a sound or word," that extends into all the world.

I've traveled to several large cities, including Chicago, New York, and London. And I'll admit, there is something special about these big cities that draws me in. I don't have the t-shirt, but I heart NY. I do. I love standing in Time Square at night and being surrounded by the LED screens and the Broadway marquees and the high-rise buildings and the bustle of busy streets. Standing there in the middle of it all, I marvel at what mankind has created, yet, at the same time, I feel no deep connection to God or to humanity. It's a magical moment, but something is missing. I feel oddly alone.

But I've also been privileged to explore God's natural world too.

I've ascended to the top of Camelback Mountain and hiked across Devil's Bridge in Arizona. I've swam among the coral reefs of the Florida Keys and Cozumel, Mexico. I've stood along the shore of Niagara Falls and paddled the whitewater of a half-dozen rivers in the southeast. I've basked at the majesty of the Canadian Rockies in Banff, Calgary, and kayaked among the mangroves of the Caribbean islands. I've walked the sandy beaches of the Atlantic, the Pacific, the Gulf of Mexico, and the Great Lakes.

And in each of those moments, I felt a deep communion with God. It was like stepping into a sanctuary and encountering the sacred.

Elizabeth Barrett Browning described it well when she wrote,

"Earth is crammed with heaven,
And every common bush afire with God,
But only he who sees takes off his shoes;
The rest sit round and pick blackberries."

There is evidence of heaven all around us in creation, and as Browning reminds us, even the "common bush is afire with God." It isn't just in the grandeur of redwood trees or a snow-covered mountain. It's in the natural world all around us.

We live in the country and my kids love to play outside. It is impossible to get them to keep their shoes on. They love to be barefoot outdoors, and I think it's because, in some unknown way, children understand what most adults have forgotten – that God is present in His creation, and we are standing on holy ground. Yes, we should take off our shoes.

The rest, Browning notes, choose to enjoy the fruit of creation with no regard for the Creator.

But Paul wrote in Romans 1,

"They know the truth about God because he has made it obvious to them. For ever since the world was created, people have seen the earth and sky. Through everything God made, they can clearly see his invisible qualities—his eternal power and divine nature. So they have no excuse for not knowing God."

Creation reveals the Creator.

In July 2021, I spent two days on a safari truck in the heart of Kenya's Serengeti National Park. When we first entered the preserve, I was giddy with excitement at seeing so many animals in their natural habitat. When I visit a zoo, I expect to see a couple of zebras or elephants. Perhaps even a lion alone in his enclosure. But there, on safari, I saw herds of zebras and elephants and antelope, hundreds of them together at a time. I was just yards from a family of cheetahs, and I took a selfie with a lion that wasn't trapped behind a glass enclosure. (I'm neither brave nor dumb, so I stayed in the truck for the photo opp.)

Here, in the middle of the Serengeti, there was no sign of human encroachment as far as the eye could see. There were no buildings, no power lines, no highways, no factories, and no piles of garbage. In that moment, I was overcome with a desire to worship God. As I surveyed this landscape, untouched and uncorrupted by human hands, I began to imagine that this is what the Garden must have been like in Genesis before the fall of man and what the Garden City will be like as we read in Revelation 21 and 22. I was witness to a glimpse of the vision for the in-between. At peace in God's good creation.

Shalom.

Paul continues in Romans 1, lamenting that "instead of worshiping the glorious, ever-living God, they worshiped idols made to look like mere people and birds and animals and reptiles."

No matter how good the technology gets, AI and virtual reality will never compare to God's created world. The world is better viewed through binoculars than our VR Goggles. We need more time with birds and less time with the bird app (a.k.a. Twitter.) More streams, less streaming.

We were created to live in a spiritual reality, not a virtual reality.

A report from 2016 found that the average cellphone user touches his or her phone 2617 times per day, and Apple found that iPhone users unlock their phones 80 times per day.[7] We need to touch the earth and the grass and the butterflies and the ladybugs more and our devices less. We need to unlock our imaginations more than our iPhones.

We weren't made to live on concrete and pavement. We need time outdoors. To breathe fresh uncirculated air. We need to bask in the warm glow of the sun and not just in the blue light of our screens.

Spend time in creation. Take a walk. Sit outside in the cool of the day. Explore your local parks.

Creation reveals the Creator. Seek shalom with God and creation.

Shalom With Others

I loved Show & Tell as a kid. You could bring just about anything you wanted to school and there would be time in the morning meeting to share it with the class. I can remember classmates that would bring toys, stuffed animals, vacation photos, and even the occasional pet hamster or turtle.

I remember in fifth grade bringing my new pocketknife to school and being allowed to open the blade and carefully show it to the rest of the class. (I don't recommend taking a knife to school for Show & Tell these days!)

The pocketknife required no explanation. It spoke for itself, drawing oohs and ahhs from my ten-year-old peers, followed by a flood of questions about where I got it and what kinds of things I would do with it. It was always show first, tell second.

I have found this to be true of our Christian witness as well.

---

[7] Julia Naftulin, "Here's how many times we touch our phones every day," Business Insider, July 13, 2016, https://www.businessinsider.com/dscout-research-people-touch-cell-phones-2617-times-a-day-2016-7.

If our Gospel only leads us to shalom with God and His creation but does not also prompt us to pursue the flourishing of others, we have failed to absorb the whole of Scripture.

John the Baptist challenged the crowds that gathered for baptism to "prove by the way that you live that you have repented of your sins and turned to God." In other words, the evidence of our relationship with God should be demonstrated by the way we live out our relationships with everyone around us.

> Don't just say to each other, 'We're safe, for we are descendants of Abraham.' That means nothing, for I tell you, God can create children of Abraham from these very stones. Even now the ax of God's judgment is poised, ready to sever the roots of the trees. Yes, every tree that does not produce good fruit will be chopped down and thrown into the fire."
>
> The crowds asked, "What should we do?"
>
> John replied, "If you have two shirts, give one to the poor. If you have food, share it with those who are hungry."
>
> Even corrupt tax collectors came to be baptized and asked, "Teacher, what should we do?"
>
> He replied, "Collect no more taxes than the government requires."
>
> "What should we do?" asked some soldiers.
>
> John replied, "Don't extort money or make false accusations. And be content with your pay."[8]

---

[8] Luke 3:7-14

We need to be good at Show & Tell. I think that would be John's message if he were delivering it today.

Live it before we lecture it.

Works before witness.

Show and tell.

John goes on to say that "every tree that doesn't bear good fruit will be chopped down" because the ax of God's judgement is ready to sever the roots.

If the fruit isn't good, then judgment happens at the roots. Why? Because there is an organic connection between the roots of the tree and the fruit that it produces.

The fruit reveals the root.

If a farmer finds bad fruit on a fruit tree, it isn't enough to just get rid of the bad fruit. In order to ensure good fruit the next time, the farmer must make changes at the root system.

In this same way, our words and actions reveal what is in our hearts.

If we don't like what we see and hear in our relationship with God or with those around us, it's not enough to simply try to change our behavior. We must start at the root level. We need a change of heart.

The fruit reveals the root.

The crowd present hears these words from John, and they come forward and begin to question him, trying to gain clarity about his true intention, asking, "what should we do?"

Isn't that our nature, too? We hear the challenging words of Scripture, and we immediately want to ask, "Yes, but what are we actually required to do?" We understand the aspiration of the Gospel message, but we also tend to look for an easy way out. Surely it doesn't really mean what it says.

John doesn't tell them to go to church, or pay their tithe, or lead a small group. He doesn't tell them to sing songs or pray harder.

John tells the crowd that if they have two shirts to give one away, and if they have food, they should share it with those who are hungry. The crowd wants to know what it looks like to live in a way that proves they have turned to God, and John gets downright practical in his advice.

Use your more-than-enough to help another's not-enough.

How do we help others to flourish? We give out of our own abundance to meet a need.

We can live generously because we know that if we give it away that God will provide more of what we need.

The corrupt tax collectors come and ask what they should do. John tells them not to collect more taxes than the government requires. Some soldiers come next and ask what they should do. John instructs them to stop extorting money and making false accusations.

The tax collectors were Jews who were tasked to collect taxes from their own people on behalf of the Roman government. These tax collectors were often corrupt, and they would add an extra charge to a Jewish man's tax bill and keep the money to line their own pockets. And the Jewish people had no recourse with the Roman government. That's just how the system worked. There was nothing that could be done about it.

In that day, soldiers could accuse innocent people of false charges and then force them to pay money to clear their name and avoid further punishment. Again, it was an accepted practice and there was little that the Jewish people could do except to pay the charges.

So when the tax collectors and the soldiers approached John and asked, what should we do? John makes it plain: stop cheating and extorting others, even when the system says you can.

Do the right thing even when the wrong thing is acceptable.

John exhorts the crowd to live justly.

Dr. Tony Evans, speaking to the NRB in 2021 said, "we cannot dismiss the Gospel by calling on the content of the Gospel that gets us to heaven while we skip over the scope of the Gospel which ought to change how we relate to one another on earth."

Show & Tell.

The evidence that we have repented of our sins and turned to God is shalom with neighbor.

Pursue peace with others.

Shalom With Self

When I was in my early twenties, I had genuinely committed to my Christian faith. But, boy was it a struggle. I felt so bad for being such a lousy Christian. I would fall to my knees in my apartment and beg God to help me to do better and to be better. I had placed my faith in Jesus and pledged my allegiance to Him, so why was I failing to live like it?

Becoming a Christian is not just a moment of conversion, but a lifetime of formation.

We see this theme repeated in the New Testament, such as in Colossians 2:6-7, when Paul writes,

"And I rejoice that you are living as you should and that your faith in Christ is strong. And now, just as you accepted Christ Jesus as your Lord, you must continue to follow him."

Paul is writing to the church of Colossae, to a group of people that he says has a faith in Christ that is strong. But then he goes on to encourage them that just as they accepted Christ Jesus as Lord, they must now continue to follow him.

The moment that we confess Christ as Lord, we become a believer. But it is a lifetime of faithfully following Jesus that truly forms us into Christians, that is, "little Christs."

Choosing Jesus as Lord is not the end of our faith journey, it is the beginning.

What does this process of maturation, of formation, of following Jesus, look like according to Paul? He continues in Colossians 2:7, "Let your roots grow down into him, and let your lives be built on him."

Paul gives us this beautiful metaphor of what it looks like to follow Jesus and it's a picture of a tree with deep roots. Paul is challenging us to let our roots grow deep down into Jesus and to let our lives be built on him.

When we see a tree with roots that go down deep into a fertile, nutrient-rich soil, we find a tree that is healthy and flourishing on the surface.

When our roots go deep into the soil Jesus, we receive all the things that we need to grow and flourish and bear good fruit.

Paul summarizes this in verse 7, noting that "then your faith will grow strong in the truth you were taught, and you will overflow with thankfulness."

Shalom with self is understanding that our identity is rooted in Jesus.

When we get that right, we will be at peace with ourselves.

When we get that wrong, we will struggle with our identity and who we want to be.

Paul challenges us to be rooted in Jesus, but then follows this encouragement with a warning:

"Don't let anyone capture you with empty philosophies and high-sounding nonsense that come from human thinking and from the spiritual powers of this world…"

In the 21ˢᵗ century, I think an apt description of "these empty philosophies and high-sounding nonsense" of which Paul warns is what Dr. Leonard Sweet called "Youniversalism."

Youniversalism says that we each get to be the center of the universe.

And it is reinforced by the more than 5000 ads and messages that we encounter every day. These form an anti-Gospel self-ology that rather than inviting us to know God, it simply invites us to be God. Our creedal confession transforms from "Jesus is Lord" to "It's all about me!"

The biggest competing philosophy to Christianity today is not post-modernism or secularism or humanism or socialism or any of the other *-isms* that we learn about in a Biblical Worldview workshop.

No, I believe that the biggest competing philosophy to Christianity today is materialism.

Materialism teaches that we need more junk. We need more stuff because stuff makes us happy. The liturgy and habits of our lives becomes that of shopping and spending. In fact, shopping is now the number one leisure activity of Americans. And these ritualistic habits shape in us a love of money, which the Bible tells us is evil.

Christianity, by contrast, offers a different perspective on the good life. We don't need more junk, we need more Jesus because our identity is rooted in Him. We don't need more shopping and spending; we instead need to pursue more serving and sharing. And these new habits will shape in us a love of neighbor, which the Bible says is the second greatest commandment.

Author Paul David Tripp wrote, "I will either get my identity vertically, from who I am in Christ, or I will shop for it horizontally in situations, experiences, and relationships of my daily life."[9]

---

[9] Paul Tripp, "Your Ministry Is Not Your Identity," Paul Tripp online, July 22, 2013, https://www.paultripp.com/articles/posts/your-ministry-is-not-your-identity.

Paul says that we are to put down deep roots in Jesus so that we pursue more of him and are formed by his love and character into a people who serve and share and express his great love to our neighbors.

When we put down deep roots in Jesus, we become anchored in our faith. When the storms come and the winds blow, we remain steadfast because of our deep roots. We may be battered by the empty philosophies or the spiritual powers of this world, but we remain unmovable in our faith. We don't waver.

Paul concludes this idea in Colossians 2:9-10, exhorting us that "for in Christ lives all the fullness of God in a human body. So you also are complete through your union with Christ…"

Your identity is rooted in Jesus. Christ completes you.

Os Guinness declared of our present day, "The age of the internet, it is said, is the age of the self and the selfie. The world is full of people full of themselves. In such an age, "I post, therefore, I am."[10]

The world tells us that more and more our identity comes from the content that we create, the digital presence we cultivate, and the online persona we are so careful to craft.

In her book, *Positivity*, author Barbara Frederickson, explains that "People who flourish function at extraordinarily high levels – both psychologically and socially. They're not simply people who feel good. Flourishing goes beyond simply happiness or satisfaction with life. Beyond feeling good, they're also doing good—adding value to the world. People who flourish are highly engaged with their families, work, and communities. They're driven by a sense of purpose: they know why they get up in the morning."[11]

For much of high school and college, I was passionate but without purpose. I was always looking for a cause to champion,

---

[10] Os Guiness, *Fool's Talk: Recovering the Art of Christian Persuasion* (Westmont: IVP, 2019).

[11] Barbara Fredrickson, *Positivity: Top-Notch Research Reveals the 3-to-1 Ratio That Will Change Your Life* (New York: Three Rivers Press, 2009), 17.

something noble to anchor my identity. My senior year of high school was the beginning of the first Gulf War, and I wore a home-made armband with a peace symbol on it to school every day and wrote essays of protest while condemning the Iraqi leader Saddam Hussein (or as I called him, "So-Damn Insane.") In college, I advocated for animal rights, becoming a vegan, refusing to wear leather, and protesting the circus each time that it came to town, marching with my "Cruelty is Not Entertainment!" placard in the parking lot. I shifted to environmentalism next, promoting reduce-reuse-recycle on our campus and covering my car with pro-environment bumper stickers.

We certainly need to be passionate about the things we believe in, but my passions were misguided because I didn't really care about animals or the environment on a deeply personal level, I just found purpose and identity in being a part of these movements.

But peace with self is understanding that our identity is rooted in Jesus and that Christ completes us.

This leads to a higher level of flourishing and a greater sense of purpose and satisfaction in life.

Nearly fifty now and I'm as passionate as ever. I'm still fighting for the things I believe in, but I'm no longer defined by them. I've given my life to the things that matter most while staying grounded in Jesus. I'm happy and content.

That's shalom.

What Is Your Shalom?

When I run into someone I know out in public, I usually start a conversation with a simple inquiry, "Hey, how's it going?" Other variations of this are typical too – "How are you?" "How are you doing?" or even the more simplistic, "What's up?"

In asking this question, we're inquiring about someone else's wellbeing. The common refrain is usually something along the lines of "I'm good" or "Not much, same old same old."

When we ask the question, we're just being courteous, aren't we? We're not really wanting or expecting the person to be open about how life is actually treating them at that moment. Even if things are falling apart, we just give a pat response – "Doing great!" – and keep the conversation moving along.

In the Jewish tradition, they would ask of one another, "What is your shalom?" This question was to inquire about the person's wellbeing by asking if they were flourishing – if they were feeling a sense of wholeness in their relationship with God, creation, others, and self.

Perhaps we could learn something from this ancient tradition by asking this question of ourselves and our family and friends. What is your shalom?

Because when we seek shalom, we find shalom.

When we create peace, we find peace.

When we put the pieces together, we discover the whole.

When we put the peaces together, we find our shalom.

CHAPTER TWO

Love Rightly

When I was seventeen and a senior in high school, I was out late one Friday night with some friends. I looked over my shoulder—for only a few short seconds—but that was long enough to lose sight of where I was. As I turned my head forward, I saw the large oak tree. But it was too late. I slammed into it at full speed.

In the immediate aftermath, I was disoriented and confused. My vision was blurry, and I found it difficult to see in the dark. The faces of the people around me were familiar, but I couldn't make sense of where we were or why we were all together in one place.

My head ached, my neck hurt, and my face was bleeding. I had suffered a concussion and a broken nose.

When I returned to school that Monday, I looked rough. I had an inch-wide scab that ran full length down the center of my face.

"What happened to you?" my classmates clamored.

"I ran into a tree."

"Oh man, that's terrible. Did you total your car?"

"No, you don't understand," I explained. "I *ran* into a tree."

Like most people who hear this story, my classmates made assumptions about what happened. They picture an automobile crash. They fill in the story to create a context that is familiar. They need it to make sense. I mean, who literally runs into a tree? There must be a car involved, right?

I believe this to be true in the Christian faith as well. We hear the invitation of Jesus to "Come, follow me," but we make assumptions about what this means, and we fill in extra details until it starts to feel familiar. We need the story to make sense to us. But what if we've gotten it wrong?

Following Jesus

Matthew 16:24-25 states, "Then Jesus said to his disciples, "If any of you wants to be my follower, you must give up your own way, take up your cross, and follow me. If you try to hang on to your life, you will lose it. But if you give up your life for my sake, you will save it."

When Jesus said this, what did he mean? When I ask this question of students in the Christian school where I work, I get responses from students like this: "Be obedient," "Follow the Ten Commandments," "Pray," "Be kind to other people," "Worship," "Read my Bible," "Try to do good things," or "Try not to do bad things."

If I were to summarize these responses in a single statement, I would say it like this: Following Jesus is about learning to live rightly.

According to this mindset, the Scriptures, then, provide us guidelines for living rightly. And so, we read the Ten Commandments, we read the Law, we read the prophets, we read Jesus' teachings, we read the Epistles. And all of these become the guidelines for how we are to live.

Growing up in church, this is what I was taught from the youngest age and what I believed it meant to follow Jesus. It was about learning to live rightly. There were certain things that Christians did, like go to church, pray before meals. And certain things Christians did not do, like use profanity or watch R-rated movies. Following Jesus meant living by an established moral code that would set me apart as a Christian.

But then as I got older, I began to wonder, is that what Jesus really meant? So, I went to the Scriptures, and I looked at what Jesus had to say, and I found this in Matthew 22:36-40:

"Teacher, which is the most important commandment in the law of Moses?"

Jesus replied, "'You must love the Lord your God with all your heart, all your soul, and all your mind.' This is the first and greatest commandment. A second is equally import-ant: 'Love your neighbor as yourself.' The entire law and all the demands of the prophets are based on these two commandments."

Jesus was asked which of the commandments is the most important and he responded that it was to love the Lord with all your heart, soul, and mind, and to love your neigh-bor as yourself. But then look at what he says next. He says, "the entire law and all the demands of the prophets are based on these two commandments."

The entirety of the law and the prophets is based on two com-mandments according to Jesus: to love God and to love people.

With this new framework in mind, that all the law and the prophets are grounded in the commands to love the Lord and to love our neighbor, to follow Jesus then is not about learning to *live* rightly, but rather to *love* rightly. The Scriptures, therefore, are not guidelines for *living*, but instead, provide us guidelines for *loving*.

As a result, even something like the Ten Commandments, which we often view as a kind of code of conduct that should be displayed in our public institutions like schools and courthouses, can be viewed as a guide for loving rightly and not simply living rightly. The first four commandments found in Exodus 20:3-8, essentially summarize for us what it looks like to love the Lord rightly:

You must not have any other god but me.

You must not make for yourself an idol of any kind or an image of anything in the heavens or on the earth or in the sea.

You must not misuse the name of the Lord your God.

Remember to observe the Sabbath day by keeping it holy.

The next six commandments recorded in verses 12-17 provide a vision for what it looks like to love our neighbor well:

Honor your father and mother.

You must not murder.

You must not commit adultery.

You must not steal.

You must not testify falsely against your neighbor.

You must not covet your neighbor's house.

I believe that everything written in the law and the prophets, all the teachings of Jesus recorded in the Gospels, and all the words of the New Testament epistles were given to us by God to help us learn how to love rightly. And loving rightly will lead us to living rightly.

You see, I don't believe that the shift to loving rightly gives us permission to do whatever we want. It's not the absence of a moral code, but rather the proper motivation for it. What I am suggesting is that if we will prioritize learning to love rightly, living rightly will be the natural consequence of our actions and will yield good fruit in our lives.

Loving and Living Rightly

In Matthew 19:16-30, we read the story about a young man who comes to Jesus with an important question:

"Teacher, what good deed must I do to have eternal life?"

"Why ask me about what is good?" Jesus replied. "There is only One who is good. But to answer your question—if you want to receive eternal life, keep the commandments."

"Which ones?" the man asked.

And Jesus replied: "'You must not murder. You must not commit adultery. You must not steal. You must not testify falsely. Honor your father and mother. Love your neighbor as yourself.'"

"I've obeyed all these commandments," the young man replied. "What else must I do?"

Jesus told him, "If you want to be perfect, go and sell all your possessions and give the money to the poor, and you will have treasure in heaven. Then come, follow me."

But when the young man heard this, he went away sad, for he had many possessions.

The young man was striving to live rightly. He told Jesus that he had kept all the commandments, but then asked, "Is there anything else that I must do?" Jesus instructs him to sell his possessions and give the money to the poor. Why would Jesus instruct him to do this? Is Jesus anti-wealth? No, I don't think so. I believe that there was something about the young man's wealth, something about his possessions, that was interfering with his ability to love rightly – either to love the Lord with all his heart or to love his neighbor as himself. Jesus tells him to get that right first, "then come follow me."

The problem when we strive to live rightly by following a set of rules, regardless of how strict they may be, is that it does not produce in us the intended godliness we desire, but self-righteousness instead. Self-righteousness is the fruit of trying to live rightly rather than love rightly.

Christlikeness & Self-Righteousness

When I was growing up, Christians were defined primarily by what they didn't do. And the ones I knew didn't smoke, dance, or watch R-rated movies. I can remember when *The Matrix* was first released in theatres. It was an R-rated film, but unlike most R-rated movies of that era, the restricted rating was because of violence, not because of sexual content or profanity. Still, it was an act of rebellion when some of the youth and college students I knew decided to go see it.

Certainly, the world has changed a lot since *The Matrix* was released in 1999, and there's less of a stigma about Christians who smoke, drink, dance, and view R-rated movies. Or get tattoos or piercings or any of the other taboo topics of my youth. But still, Christians today are largely defined by things wholly unrelated to the Scriptures.

Why do so few in the church look and act like Jesus?

There was a Barna study[12] done several years ago where they looked at American Christians and examined both their attitudes and actions to see if they reflected Christlikeness or self-righteousness. Barna surveyed people who identified as Christians and attended church on Sundays and asked them to respond to a series of statements with either "agree" or "disagree." Those statements reflected either a Christlike attitude or a self-righteous attitude, either Christlike actions or self-righteous actions. Based on their responses, Barna placed the respondents into one of four categories:

1. Self-righteous attitude + Christlike actions

This is a group of Christians who are doing the right things for all the wrong reasons. Their motivation for doing good is not rooted in a commitment to follow the ways of Jesus to love our neighbor. 14 % of respondents fell into this category.

2. Christlike attitude + self-righteous actions

This group holds the right beliefs, but their lives are either bearing bad fruit or no fruit at all. There is a disconnect between what they say and what they live out as a demonstration of their commitment to follow Jesus. 21% of respondents were included in this category.

---

[12] "Christians: More Like Jesus or Pharisees?" Barna Group, June 3, 2013, https://www.barna.com/research/christians-more-like-jesus-or-pharisees/.

So, 35% of Christians in this survey are living divided, with attitudes and actions that are segmented between being like Christ and being like a Pharisee.

3. Self-righteous attitude + self-righteous actions

This group of people who identify as Christians have attitudes and actions that would be defined as self-righteous. 51% of respondents fall into this category. If the survey participants are an accurate reflection of the church at large, then half of American Christians look and act more like modern-day Pharisees than followers of Jesus.

4. Christlike attitude + Christlike actions

Only 14% of respondents answered affirmatively to questions that reflect both Christlike attitudes and Christlike actions. Could it be because most of us have been raised to believe that following Jesus is about learning to live rightly, that there is a set of rules that we must follow, and that the Bible is that set of rules to live the right way? And just in case the Bible wasn't clear enough, most churches add more rules to further explain what they think the Bible meant.

A Code of Conduct

At our school, we have a student handbook. Every school has one of these. The front half of the handbook typically outlines all the policies and procedures, such as the start time for the school day, where to go for lunch, and what to do if you're absent. But then, the back half of the student handbook contains what is usually referred to as a code of conduct. It's pages and pages and pages of all the things you can do and can't do in a school.

And honestly, as the head of a Christian school, I would love to be able to just rip out this whole section, throw it aside, and replace it with two simple statements: love God and love people. Because if we could truly embrace these two ideals—love God and love people—we wouldn't have need of a massive volume of a code of conduct. Some might argue that I'm being ridiculous. The code of conduct includes topics like cheating. What does cheating have to do with loving God and loving people? Well, if you have a genuine love for your teacher, you don't deceive her into thinking you know something that you don't know. If you have a genuine love for other people, you know how to conduct yourself around them in honoring ways. You see, everything comes back to your ability to love God and to love people.

In Luke 6:43-45, Jesus gives this illustration:

A good tree can't produce bad fruit, and a bad tree can't produce good fruit. A tree is identified by its fruit. Figs are never gathered from thornbushes, and grapes are not picked from bramble bushes. A good person produces good things from the treasury of a good heart, and an evil person produces evil things from the treasury of an evil heart. What you say flows from what is in your heart.

Jesus uses an illustration of a tree because there is an organic connection between the roots of a tree and the fruit that it bears. And the same thing is true for you and me. There's an organic connection between our heart and the fruit that we bear, our words and our actions.

Paul Tripp tells an imaginative tale of a man who had an apple tree in his backyard, but it wasn't producing any good apples. Wanting to make his wife happy, the man went down to the home improvement store, got himself a ladder, a pneumatic nail gun and a bushel of apples. He returned home, climbed up on the ladder and cut down all the old rotten apples and began to nail the new red apples he bought at the store to the tree's limbs. Did he create a good fruit-bearing apple tree? No, he only created the appearance of one. And as Tripp notes, the tree will continue to bear bad fruit next year because nothing has been done to improve the root system of the tree.[13]

In the same way, much of Christian discipleship today—what we do in our homes, what we do in our Christian schools and youth groups, and what we do in our churches—is really nothing more than apple nailing.

It seems we're better at creating pharisees than followers. In large part because we've made following Jesus about learning to live rightly rather than love rightly. Striving only to live rightly is akin to nailing apples to a tree. When following Jesus is about learning to love rightly, we learn to deal with the issues of the heart. And that leads to transformation.

A New Commandment

John Chapter 13 records the story of the Last Supper. Jesus has washed his disciples' feet. He's announced that Judas is going to betray him. In his final moments with his disciples, he says to them in verses 34-35: "So now I am giving you a new commandment: Love each other. Just as I have loved you, you should love each other. Your love for one another will prove to the world that you are my disciples."

Jesus gives them a new commandment. He takes the original commandment—love your neighbor as yourself—and adds a new twist. We are to no longer just love our neighbor, but now we are to love "each other." Who is that? Well, that would be everybody. It

---

[13] Paul Tripp, "Getting to the Heart of Your Words," Paul Tripp online, March 31, 2017, https://www.paultripp.com/articles/posts/getting-to-the-heart-of-your-words.

would be our family, our friends, and our church community. The people who look like us and act like us.

But "each other" would also include the people who don't look like us. It's the black, the white, the Hispanic, the Asian, the Jew, the Hindu, the Muslim, the secularist, the humanist, and the atheist. It's the straight, the gay, the transgendered, the poor, the homeless, and the imprisoned. It's everyone. It's the person that voted for the other party and the person that refuses to vote for anybody.

Jesus' new commandment is to love each other, but not simply "as yourself," but "as I have loved you." We must learn to love others—the ones we like and the ones we don't—the way that Jesus loves us. He said it is this willingness to love rightly that will prove to the world that we are followers of Jesus.

How do we do it? We're empowered by the Holy Spirit, and we have God's Word to guide us. The more we will study the Scriptures, the more we will embrace the teachings of Jesus, the more we will understand his great love for us, the better we will be able to love other people the way that he loves us.

Self-Love & Self-Esteem

One of the great philosophers of the 20th century, Whitney Houston, taught us to love ourselves because to do so is, in fact, the greatest love. I call her a philosopher because she was a voice of an entire generation, and she communicated to millions of people this popular idea about the virtue of self-love. My generation grew up with this and the message has resonated with each generation since. The greatest form of love is self-love; hence we all need to first learn to love ourselves before we can love others.

Jesus talked about the greatest form of love also, but Jesus described it this way in John 15:13, "There is no greater love than to lay down one's life for one's friends." According to Jesus, sacrificial love is greater than self-love because the more that you love your-self, the less likely you are to lay down your life for another.

I was also raised in the self-esteem generation, where high self-esteem was deemed a necessary part of healthy personal development. We need to learn to hold ourselves in high regards as a part of our journey toward self-love.

Here's a little pop quiz. Do you know which group of people has the highest self-esteem?

A) Professional athletes
B) Political leaders
C) Wealthy business owners
D) University professors

The right answer is (E) None of the above. The group of people with the highest self-esteem are narcissists and sociopaths. Some of the greatest atrocities in human history were committed by people with high self-esteem. They thought so highly of themselves, they had no regard for other people.

The opposite of high self-esteem is not low self-esteem, but no self-esteem. We are not supposed to think little of ourselves, we're not supposed to think of ourselves much at all. The Apostle Paul said it this way in Philippians 2:3-4, "Don't be selfish; don't try to impress others. Be humble, thinking of others as better than yourselves. Don't look out only for your own interests, but take an interest in others, too."

If Jesus had been committed to self-love and self-esteem, would he have gone to the cross for you and me? Paul explores this theme in verses 5-8 as he considers our responsibility to emulate Christ in this way:

You must have the same attitude that Christ Jesus had.
Though he was God,

he did not think of equality with God
as something to cling to.
Instead, he gave up his divine privileges;
he took the humble position of a slave
and was born as a human being,
When he appeared in human form,
he humbled himself in obedience to God
and died a criminal's death on a cross.

Giving Grace

Have you ever seen the character from the movie *We're the Millers* with the tattoo on his chest that reads, "NO RAGRETS"? Bold move, for sure. I have a small tattoo on my left wrist of an infinity symbol with my wife's initials and our wedding date. We got these matching tattoos to celebrate on our 20th wedding anniversary in 2020. I also have a large tattoo that covers most of my right forearm that features a cross and a garden and the words, "Making All Things New."

If I were going to get a new tattoo, you know what I'd get? I think I'd go bold like No Ragrets Guy and get Colossians 3:13 tattooed on my forehead: "Make allowance for each other's faults and forgive anyone who offends you. Remember, the Lord forgave you, so you must forgive others."

Can you see it? MAKE ALLOWANCE in big bold letters right across my forehead. Why? Because I need everyone in my life to be reminded to make allowances for my faults. I need my wife, my children, my co-workers, my friends, my in-laws, and my church community among others to have a visual reminder that I will need them to make allowances for my faults because I certainly have a few of them.

We must make allowances, and then we must choose to forgive those who offend us because the Lord has forgiven us. C.S. Lewis said, "Being a Christian means forgiving the inexcusable in others because God has forgiven the inexcusable in us."

The very definition of grace assumes that the other person is not being gracious. It stops being grace altogether if it's conditional on some reciprocal gesture by the other person. Grace is not a transaction if it's two-way. We must learn to forgive unconditionally. That means we must be willing to forgive without an apology. What if they never say I'm sorry? What if they hurt your feelings? What if they say something mean? What if they do something that offends you and they never apologize? Will you still choose to forgive? What if they double down on their offensive act and do it again?

Giving grace means being willing to forgive without retribution. What if they never make it right? What if they borrow your gaming device and break it and don't get it fixed? What if they say something hurtful about you on social media and they never go on there and correct it and make it right.

Giving grace means being willing to forgive without justice. What if they never get punished? This one's hard. I sit with a lot of students and their parents who have a hard time letting go of the offense until I've assured them that the offender has been punished. As soon as they know that the other student has been suspended or expelled, then they're settled, but not until. We have a hard time choosing to forgive without justice, but the Bible says that we are to forgive without condition, and that includes seeking justice.

A few years ago, I had a friend who had something happen to one of his sons. He was very upset, and he made some threatening statements that I knew he would come to regret. I reached out to him over the course of that day, but we never connected. That night, I felt prompted by the Holy Spirit to reach out to him. So, I drove to his house at ten o'clock at night. I stood in his driveway and called his phone and asked him to come outside.

As soon as he came out of the house, he became animated, demanding, "Do you know what they did to my son?"

I replied, "You're telling me the story of a father who's upset because his son was unjustly mistreated by others. That sounds familiar. That sounds like the gospel. And you know how God responded in that situation. Your sins against his son are far greater than what has been done to your son. God chose to forgive. You have no choice but to forgive also."

When it comes down to it, we either believe it or we don't. We either choose to forgive or we don't. But we can't continue to follow Jesus while we hold tightly to our unforgiveness because we didn't get the apology we expected, the retribution we deserved, or the justice we demanded. Spoken Word artist Hosanna Poetry writes that "grace is the greatest brave." Grace takes courage. Grace takes bravery.

As Jesus hung on the cross, he could have called down an army of angels to rescue him from that cross. But even with that at his disposal, the weapon that he chose to fight with was grace. Romans 5:8 says, "But God showed his great love for us by sending Christ to die for us while we were still sinners." Before we could make an apology and say, "I'm sorry, forgive me," and before we could think about retribution and how we might try to make it right, Jesus chose grace and forgiveness. He could have demanded justice, but instead, he chose the way of love. If Jesus was willing to forgive us without apology, retribution, or an expectation of justice, how much more should we be willing to do that for one another?

I have a friend who published her memoir, entitled *Iridescent Grace*. It's the story of the most horrific childhood you could possibly ever imagine—abused, neglected, nearly killed by her own mother, and an eyewitness to her father's murder in her home. And yet, if you met her today, you'd discover a woman who is full of joy, full of hope, and full of life. In her book, she writes,

I learned that when someone owes a debt he cannot pay, I carry it until I forgive him and give up the debt. If I forgive him but hold on to the debt, I have to keep forgiving him every time he comes to mind. To completely rid myself of the burden, I have to forgive the offender and give his debt to Jesus, who accepts the debt, pays it with his sacrifice at the cross, and sets me free from it. I receive from Jesus what was owed by the offender. My forgiving the offender gets me out of the picture. It doesn't let the offender off the hook with God. It removes me as judge. It gives God his rightful place as judge.[14]

It was a camping trip, and we were playing football late that night in a nearby park. It was dark and we were relying on the moon and the stars and a light pole in an adjacent parking lot to be able to see. I was lined up at receiver. The ball was snapped, and I used a double move to get by my defender. The quarterback had thrown the ball deep. I looked over my shoulder—for only a few short seconds—but that was long enough to lose sight of where I was. As the ball hit my hands and I secured the catch, I turned my head and saw the large oak tree in my path. But it was too late. I slammed into it at full speed.

In the immediate aftermath, I was disoriented and confused. I was laying on the ground with people standing over me. My first thought was, "you might have a concussion, don't pass out." So instead, I jumped to my feet and started pacing around. My vision was blurry, and I found it difficult to see in the dark. I was wearing eyeglasses that night and they had flown off my face when I hit the tree. A friend found them and returned them. I put them on, and everything came back into focus. The faces of the people around

---

[14] Carly Richaven, *Iridescent Grace: The Journey from Pain to Pearls* (Bloomington: WestBow Press, 2016), 24.

me were familiar, but I couldn't make sense of where we were or why we were all together in one place.

But I didn't go home that night. No, even with a broken nose and a mild concussion and a serious case of whiplash, I stayed on through the weekend campout.

The quarterback who threw the pass that led me right into the tree? My stepdad.

The ones closest to us are often the ones that hurt us most, even when they don't mean to.

What do we offer in exchange? Forgiveness.

Grace takes courage. And I've got the crooked nose to prove it.

CHAPTER THREE

Go Further

I was sitting in a middle school classroom when we heard the gunshots exploding just down the hall. We hid under our desks and waited. Waited for the gunman to find us and shoot us.

The gunfire grew louder. The door flew open. The gunman stood over me and yelled, "Look at me!" I looked up at the barrel of the gun. He pulled the trigger. The gun exploded and the bullet struck me in the chest. I was dead. Another victim of a school shooting.

Fortunately, this was just a drill. The gunman was an officer from the local police department and that scenario was staged so that we could experience the helplessness of hiding and waiting as a response to an active shooter. The small plastic yellow bullet from the airsoft gun that had struck me in the chest stung for a minute but faded. The memory did not. I still have that bullet in my desk drawer as a reminder of that moment.

I left that training exercise certified as an instructor, authorized to go back to my school and train my teachers on how to properly respond to active shooter scenarios on our campus. But those two days in a room full of law enforcement officers from across our region gave me a new resolve. As a follower of Jesus, I didn't only want to prevent school shootings. I also wanted to prevent school shooters.

Deeper In, Further Out

1 John 4:17 states, "And as we live in God, our love grows more perfect. So we will not be afraid on the day of judgment, but we can face him with confidence because we live like Jesus here in this world."

The Apostle John said that as we grow in God, our love is made perfect. What love? In the context of the verses that precede it, we can infer that John is speaking of our love of neighbor. I would suggest that as Christians, we are to live a life that is deeper in and further out.[15] As we go deeper with God, our love for others will extend further out.

Cultural influences instruct us to follow our hearts. This is a common theme in the music that we listen to and the shows and movies that we watch. But the Bible tells us in Proverbs 4:23, "Guard your heart above all else, for it determines the course of your life."

In other words, what you love is what you will live. So rather than following our heart, the Bible instructs us that we should lead our heart. Our hearts need leadership under the submission to the Holy Spirit, because if we follow our hearts, our heart's desires will take us to a place that we don't want to go.

Philosophers use the Greek word *telos* to describe our chief aim in life, that thing that we aspire towards, the source of our loves, our desires, and our picture of the good life. We can think of it like the bullseye on a target. It's that thing that we're aiming to hit. Imagine an archer as he pulls back his bow and draws his arrow. He uses his sight to make subtle adjustments to bring his arrow into alignment

---

[15] I was introduced to the phrase "Deeper In, Further Out" by my friends at Hamilton District Christian High School.

with the target. When he is ready, he steadies his breathing, releases the arrow, and watches as it hits the target.

The same is true for our Christian formation. It is that process of perfecting in our lives. It is about making the adjustments, about bringing our heart into alignment with what the Bible says our telos, our target, should be—a love of God and a love of people. Everything that we do as Christians—our worship, prayer, Bible reading, and gatherings—is all designed to bring our heart's desires into alignment with a love of God and a love of people.

Missing the Mark

But sometimes we miss the mark. This is one of the literal translations of the word sin. To sin is to miss the mark. There are moments in our lives when we are aligned towards the love of God and the love of people and something distracts us, something disrupts us, and we miss the mark. We commit sin, not as the breaking of a kind of moral code, but in missing the mark in our love of God or our love of others.

If the two great commandments are to love God and to love others, then it follows that the two great sins in the world are idolatry and injustice. Not loving the Lord our God with all our hearts (idolatry) and not loving our neighbor as ourselves (injustice). To miss the mark is to be guilty of idolatry or injustice.

In that active shooter response training, we learned about a tactical strategy called the OODA Loop. *OODA* is an acronym that stands for Observe, Orient, Decide, and Act. It's a looping process that we all go through in our daily activities. When we walk or when we drive, we are constantly observing, orienting, deciding, and taking action. It's a repeated cycle that we do in all the activities that we participate in. Because of that, a tactical strategy that can be used against an assailant is to interrupt his OODA loop. In a school setting where there are students or adults trapped in a classroom and a shooter is making entry, rather than passively hiding under a desk, staff are taught to interrupt the OODA loop. The moment the shooter enters the classroom, everyone is instructed to throw things at him—the stapler, textbooks, a laptop, backpacks, whatever is available. When this happens, the shooter's natural reaction is to guard his face and protect his head which temporarily halts his ability to accurately fire his weapon. His OODA loop has been interrupted. In that moment, he can be pushed to the ground and subdued or shoved out of the way for students and staff to escape the classroom to safety.

The same thing happens in our Christian formation. Our loves are properly aligned towards God and neighbor, but then something suddenly interrupts our OODA loop and causes us to miss the mark. Sometimes there are simple distractions like our family, our social media, our cable news channel, our jobs, or our health that we must learn to manage. And sometimes there are besetting sins that become real disruptions that we must find ways to eliminate.

The writer of Hebrews instructs us in Chapter 12, verse 2, "let us strip off every weight that slows us down, especially the sin that so easily trips us up. And let us run with endurance the race God has set before us."

What distractions do you need to manage? It might be certain music that you listen to. It might be certain social media channels that you pay attention to. It might be certain people that you surround yourself with. And what disruptions do you need to eliminate? What habitual sins are causing you to miss the mark? Maybe it's lust or anger or jealousy or arrogance. Whatever it may be, these interruptions in our spiritual OODA loop provide new opportunities to realign our hearts toward a love of God and a love of neighbor.

Love of Neighbor

1 John 4:20 states, "If someone says, "I love God," but hates his brother, that person is a liar; for if we don't love people we can see, how can we love God, whom we cannot see?" Simply put, I believe that the evidence of our love of God is our love of neighbor.

When Jesus was asked, "who is my neighbor?" He answered with the parable of the Good Samaritan. The hero of Jesus' story is not the religious elite, as neither the priest nor the Levite stops to help the man who was beaten and robbed and left to die on the side of the road. No, the unlikely hero is the traveler from Samaria, a man whom the Jews would have considered ethnically inferior and a half-breed. By elevating the Samaritan as the heroic figure, Jesus cannot be any clearer in defining "my neighbor." Our neighbors are not simply the people around us that we look like and act like and live next door to. Our neighbor is also the person we see as less than us. The person we want to avoid. The person in need that everybody else ignores. A person that is going to require something of us. Perhaps something sacrificial. They are also our neighbors.

John concludes in verse 21, "And he has given us this command: Those who love God must also love his brother." Yes, we demonstrate our love of God through our worship, our prayers, and our service, but the evidence of our love of God is our love of neighbor.

Getting Even

In Matthew 5:43, Jesus proclaims, "You have heard the law that says, 'Love your neighbor' and hate your enemy. But I say, love your enemies! Pray for those who persecute you!"

If the evidence of our love of God is our love of neighbor, then I would suggest that the evidence of our love of neighbor is our love of enemy.

This is hard for us because we love getting revenge. Especially in America, and even in the church, we love vengeance. It's a wildly popular genre for making movies and writing books. There's almost never a time when you can't find a blockbuster movie about vengeance playing in theaters. We love them. We celebrate them.

"Hello. My name is Inigo Montoya. You killed my father. Prepare to die." When Montoya finally kills the six-fingered man and avenges his father's death in *The Princess Bride*, we cheer.

We root for thieves and robbers to commit great crimes because we decide the person being victimized somehow deserves it. Hence the popularity of *Ocean's 11* that led to the spin-offs of *Ocean's 12*, *Ocean's 13*, and later the all-female version of *Ocean's 8*.

We love the revenge genre because we love when people get what's coming to them. And that's nothing new. The Bible has a long history of vengeance, and it goes all the way back to Genesis when Cain killed his brother Abel. And then just a few generations later, we meet Lamech who said,

I have killed a man who attacked me,
 a young man who wounded me.
If someone who kills Cain is punished seven times,
then the one who kills me will be punished seventy-seven times!

In the span of four generations, vengeance has gone from seven-times to seventy-seven times.

When the law is given in Exodus 21, we see vengeance addressed in verses 23-25:

But if there is further injury, the punishment must match the injury: a life for a life, an eye for an eye, a tooth for a tooth, a hand for a hand, a foot for a foot, a burn for a burn, a wound for a wound, and a bruise for a bruise.

The law is not an endorsement of vengeance so much as it's an attempt to rein it in. It's no longer seventy-seven times, but one-for-one. What you do to me, I can do to you.

But Jesus addresses this in Matthew 5:38-41 when he reminded the people,

> You have heard the law that says the punishment must match the injury: 'An eye for an eye, and a tooth for a tooth.' But I say, do not resist an evil person! If someone slaps you on the right cheek, offer the other cheek also. If you are sued in court and your shirt is taken from you, give your coat, too. If a soldier demands that you carry his gear for a mile, carry it two miles.

In no uncertain terms, Jesus states in his Sermon on the Mount that the long history of vengeance comes to an end with his kingdom. In Luke 4, we read the story of Jesus when he goes into the temple, and he's given the opportunity to read from the Scriptures. He's handed the scroll of Isaiah, and he unrolls it until he finds these words and begins to read aloud:

> The Spirit of the Lord is upon me,
> for he has anointed me to bring Good News to the poor.
> He has sent me to proclaim that captives will be released,
> that the blind will see,
> that the oppressed will be set free,
> and that the time of the Lord's favor has come.

And then he stopped, sat down, and said, "The Scripture you've just heard has been fulfilled this very day!"

As Pastor Brian Zahnd notes, those in the synagogue would have noticed something was missing.[16] They would have known that Jesus stopped one line too early, that there wasn't a period after the last word, but that there was one more line.

The text Jesus was quoting in Isaiah 61 reads,

> that the time of the Lord's favor has come,
> and with it, the day of God's anger against their enemies.

Jesus makes clear to all in the temple that day that there will be no day of vengeance in the kingdom of heaven. And to leave no doubt, he continues by reminding the people of two stories of God's mercy toward their enemies – the widow of Zarephath and Namaan the Syrian. During the famine, Elijah was sent to a widow in the land of Sidon, the land of Jezebel and worshippers of Baal. Though there were many lepers in Israel, God sent Elisha to heal Namaan, a commander in an enemy army.

Luke tells us that the people became so angry that they drove Jesus outside and tried to throw him off a cliff. As Zahnd concludes, "It's amazing just how angry some people can become if you try to take away their religion of revenge."

And Jesus said there will be no more vengeance.

In Romans 12:19-20, Paul writes,

> Dear friends, never take revenge. Leave that to the righteous anger of God. For the Scriptures say,

> "I will take revenge;
> I will pay them back,"
> says the Lord.

---

[16] Brian Zahnd, "Closing the Book on Vengeance," Brian Zahnd online, January 30, 2016, https://brianzahnd.com/2016/01/closing-the-book-on-vengeance/.

Instead,

"If your enemies are hungry, feed them.
 If they are thirsty, give them something to drink.
In doing this, you will heap
burning coals of shame on their heads."
Don't let evil conquer you, but conquer evil by doing good.

As followers of Jesus, we're not supposed to feed our anger, we're supposed to feed our enemies. But we have a long history in America and in the church of feeding our anger and outing our enemies.

When I was ten years old, I had a scuffle with a childhood friend who lived next door. We had been playing in my front yard when something happened—I have no idea what—and tempers flared. We ended up in a skirmish, mostly pushing and shoving before he ran off. He was about twenty feet away when he turned back and yelled at me. Without a moment's pause, I bent down, picked up a rock from our dirt driveway, spun around, and threw it as hard as I could in his direction. That jagged rock hit him square in the forehead and he dropped to the ground. When he staggered back to his feet, his face was covered in blood. I rushed inside to tell my mom. She tended to his wound before taking him to his house and apologetically explained to his family that I was not, in fact, a raging lunatic. Sadly, our thirst for vengeance begins at a young age.

Thieves and Robbers

In charismatic circles, it's not uncommon to hear people describe a difficult season or a challenging moment as a spiritual attack by the devil because "the thief does not come except to steal, and to kill, and to destroy."[17] In doing so, they cite the words of Jesus, but miss his point.

In John 10:7-10, Jesus says,

> "I tell you the truth, I am the gate for the sheep. All who came before me were thieves and robbers. But the true sheep did not listen to them. Yes, I am the gate. Those who come in through me will be saved. They will come and go freely and will find good pastures. The thief's purpose is to steal and kill and destroy. My purpose is to give them a rich and satisfying life.

The Old Testament prophecies painted two pictures of what the coming Messiah was going to look like – a conquering king and a suffering servant. The Jews were waiting for a Messiah that would rise to power and violently overthrow Roman rule and establish a new kingdom where they would be in power, and their oppression would be avenged. As a result, they failed to see the Messiah in Jesus the suffering servant.

When Jesus said, "all who came before me were thieves and robbers," he is referring to the other messianic figures of his day. There were other people at that time who also claimed to be the Messiah before Jesus and history records many of them.[18]

One of them was Judas, son of Hezekiah. The historian Josephus called him "head of the robbers." Four years before Jesus' birth, he assaulted a royal palace in Galilee near Nazareth, seized weapons, stole money, and terrorized the countryside until he was finally put down by the Roman army.

In the early years of Jesus' childhood, there was a messianic claim by Simon of Peraea. Simon was a servant of Herod who

---

[17] John 10:10 (NKJV)

[18] James Tabor, "Messiahs in the Time of Jesus," James Tabor online, April 12, 2019, https://jamestabor.com/messiahs-in-the-time-of-jesus/.

became king after Herod's death. He burned and ransacked several royal palaces until Herod's former commander assembled an army to stop Simon. He was caught and beheaded.

A few years later, Judas the Galilean stirred up a revolt until they were brutally crushed by the Roman army. Josephus reports that 2000 people were crucified in the aftermath.

These men, and others like them, are the thieves and robbers of which Jesus speaks. When he warns that "the thief's purpose is to steal and kill and destroy," the thief he speaks of is not the devil. The word in the Greek is *klepto* not *diabolos*; thief, not devil. It is the false messiahs—the thieves and robbers—who sought a violent means to establish a new kingdom whose way leads to death and destruction.

In contrast to the death and destruction offered by these thieves and robbers, Jesus said, "my purpose is to give them a rich and satisfying life." In other words, following the nonviolent, peaceful way of Jesus is what leads us to a rich and satisfying life. We don't receive the abundant life by only choosing Jesus. We receive the abundant life by also choosing the ways of Jesus. It's the peaceful co-suffering, co-loving ways of Jesus that leads us to a rich and satisfying life.

We can't harbor anger and unforgiveness and have the abundant life. We can't hate our black, brown, Asian, Muslim, Jewish, LGBTQ+ brothers and sisters and have the abundant life. We can't call for revenge against our enemies and those who stand against us and have a rich and satisfying life. We can't choose political expediency at the expense of those who will suffer more and have the abundant life. It is only by the peaceful, nonviolent ways of Jesus that we experience a rich and satisfying life.

As Jesus hung on the cross, he cried out, "Father, forgive them, for they don't know what they are doing."[19] In his violent, excruciating death, when he had every justification to exact revenge for

---

[19] Luke 23:34

an unjust crime, Jesus still chose the way of forgiveness. Even as he suffered in crucifixion, Jesus chose to be an advocate and not an accuser, setting the example from his mandate the day before, "Just as I have loved you, you should love each other." Will we choose to be an advocate or an accuser?

Seeking Justice

But I can hear the critics already, "This is crazy! You're suggesting that we do nothing about the evils in our world?" Of course not. God commands us to be agents of justice in the world, to be a voice for the voiceless, to care for the widows and the orphans, and to free the oppressed. We are commanded and commissioned to do this, but we can do it in a peaceful, nonviolent way.

Jesus instructed us to turn the other cheek, not to turn a blind eye. We don't ignore injustice. We choose to respond to it differently.

There are two types of justice that we can pursue. The first is retributive justice. Retributive justice says, "I will not be satisfied until somebody is punished." We love this kind of justice. This is the kind of justice that prompts us to exclaim, "Lock them up and throw away the key!" "Let's throw the book at them!" "We need to prosecute them to the fullest extent of the law!" "I hope they rot in prison!"

But there's another kind of justice we can pursue and that is restorative justice. Restorative justice says, "I will not be satisfied until you are made well." It may mean for their safety or for the safety of the community, that they will have to be removed from the community for a time, but we do not stop hoping and working to see them restored.

We see an illustration of this type of justice in the parable of the Prodigal Son, recorded in Luke Chapter 15. Jesus tells the story of a Jewish son who asks his father for his inheritance. He takes his inheritance, leaves home, and squanders it among the Gentiles in extravagant living. Eventually, he finds himself eating with pigs and realizes that even his father's servants live better than this. He decides to return home and beg his father to let him be a servant in his house.

So far, this would not have been a new story for Jesus' audience, but rather a simple retelling of a familiar tale in Jewish culture. In the traditional telling of the story, the young man would have returned home, and the community would have gathered around him for a Kezazah ceremony.[20] They would have smashed a ceramic pot at his feet, signifying that he has been cut off. It was a source of public shame and mockery, and the intent was clear – the relationship is broken and beyond repair and the young man is no longer welcomed.

But Jesus changed the ending.

When Jesus announces that when the father sees his son from afar, the father runs to him, a significant plot twist is introduced. Why does the father run? Because he knows that he must get to his son before the community does, because he knows what the community has in store. The father runs to his son, and he receives him and embraces him and says, "We must celebrate with a feast, for this son of mine was dead and has now returned to life. He was lost, but now he is found."[21] The father's response to his son's return is not a ceremony, but a celebration. He puts a ring and a robe on his son to communicate to all those who have gathered that they can all take their ceramic pots and go home. There will be no cutting off ceremony today.

In the story, Jesus says that the father ran, which is an interesting detail because Jewish men didn't run. To run while wearing a robe required a man to pull up his robe and expose his legs, something

---

[20] David Devenish, "The Prodigal Son," David Devenish online, 2016, https://daviddevenish.com/portfolio/the-prodigal-son/.

[21] Luke 15:24

that would have been shameful to do. The father chose restorative justice for his son and was willing to endure shame to meet his son and receive him back. Are we willing to endure shame to ensure that somebody that the community wants to cut off can be restored instead?

Or are we more like the jealous older brother who will only settle for retribution? We tend towards this worrisome fear that people will get away with wrongdoing. The community believed that unless the young man was cut off, there would be no punishment. Yet, I'd argue that the prodigal son didn't get away with anything. He lost his inheritance. He lived without food and family for a season. He was likely shamed by his community when he returned home despite his father's efforts. I'd say the prodigal son was punished enough.

Anytime we go against the command to love and live as Jesus instructed, we suffer the very real consequences of our actions. Paul described it this way in Romans 6:23, "For the wages of sin is death." I don't think that Paul intended this as solely a statement about eternity. The consequences of missing the mark in any area of our lives results in a kind of death. Nobody gets away with anything, even if some outside authority never executes justice.

The Second Coming

But what about when Jesus comes back? He's coming back for vengeance, right?

Revelation 19:11-15 states,

Then I saw heaven opened, and a white horse was standing there. Its rider was named Faithful and True, for he judges fairly and wages a righteous war. His eyes were like flames of fire, and on his head were many crowns. A name was written on him that no one understood except himself. He wore a robe dipped in blood, and his title was the Word of God. The armies of heaven, dressed in the finest of pure white linen, followed him on white horses. From his mouth came a sharp sword to strike down the nations.

Yes, when Jesus returns, he is coming with a sword. But the sword is in his mouth, not in his hand, because he is the "Word of God," and it is the word of God that will cause the nations to bow.

If we are going to wield a sword, let it be in our mouths, and let it be the word of God.

Hurt People, Hurt People

I don't pretend to understand the specific motivations behind school shootings. I know that there are no simple explanations and that there is a growing body of literature exploring the causes of this horrific phenomenon. I can give time and effort to learning to prepare for a school shooting. But I'd rather give time and effort to learning to live and love in a way that means there will be fewer school shootings. This much I know: hurt people hurt people. In the aftermath of a school shooting, we begin to see what we failed to see before – the signs that something was amiss.

In his Tedx Talk, "I Was Almost a School Shooter," Aaron Stark shares of his tragic upbringing, riddled with abuse, neglect, and homelessness. Mired in a darkness and without hope, he purchased a gun and was preparing a violent end to his life at his high school. Until he met a friend. And even though Aaron had stolen from this friend and ruined some of his belongings, the friend continued to show Aaron kindness. Aaron shares,

When someone treats you like you are a person when you don't even feel like you're human, it will change your entire world, and it did to me. He stopped me with his acts of kindness from committing that atrocity that day.[22]

Today, Aaron is happily married and a father to four children. That friend who saved him? They're still friends to this day. The lesson that Aaron wants us all to learn from his experience is captured in the final line of his talk: "Love the ones you feel deserve it the least because they need it the most." Can we love in a way that reaches the unlovable, the bullied, the neglected, the marginalized, and the outcast?

Following Jesus is about living deeper in and further out. The deeper we go in God, the more our love is perfected and the further out it begins to grow. Our love moves beyond our family and our friends, and our *telos* becomes a transcendent love of neighbor for those we don't know and those we don't like. And perhaps one day, we'll be ready to put away our ceramic pots.

---

[22] Aaron Stark, "I Was Almost a School Shooter," YouTube Video, June 26, 2018, Tedx Boulder, https://www.youtube.com/watch?v=azRl1dI-Cts.

CHAPTER FOUR

Do Something

In 2018, I met Tara for the first time. She was homeless and pregnant. I gave her some money. A year later, she gave me her son.

It was a Thursday night, and we had decided to grab dinner at a local restaurant because my wife and I were simply too tired to cook. We had worked late at school and our five kids were all hungry. After devouring about 100 chicken wings and fries, we paid the check and loaded up to drive home. My wife had the kids in her minivan. I drove separately. We pulled out of the parking lot and were sitting at the red light waiting impatiently to turn left onto the main highway and head home after a very long day. My family had pulled up alongside me at the traffic light.

In my side mirror, I noticed the driver getting out of the car behind me which is an odd thing to do at an intersection. She ran past my driver's door into the median, and I followed her with my gaze. What the heck is she doing? Then I saw the cardboard sign with the handwritten letters. PREGNANT AND HOMELESS. Now I understood. The driver had jumped out her car and was giving the disheveled teen her leftovers. I quickly pulled my wallet out of my pocket to look for some cash, but I didn't have any. My wife saw the girl and saw me looking in my wallet and realized what I was doing. She found some cash in her purse, rolled down her window, gestured for me to roll down my window, and threw a pair of ten-dollar bills onto my passenger seat. I grabbed the cash, rolled down my driver's side window and extended the money out to the young mom-to-be. She stood up awkwardly, hand on her belly, walked over, and took the money from my hand. She offered a quiet thank you without ever looking up. She returned to her seat in the median as the light turned green and I pulled out onto the highway. It had been a very long day and I could not wait to get home.

But God had other plans. I wasn't even a hundred yards down the road when I heard the spirit of God say to me, "You can do better."

"God, I just gave her all the cash we have on us."

"You can do better."

With a deep sigh of resignation, I called my wife and told her to turn around. We were going to revisit the pregnant teen and see how God might be directing us.

We did a U-turn at the next signal and then pulled into a coffee shop's parking lot nearby. We walked over to the girl in the median and introduced ourselves.

"Hi, I'm Jim, and this is my wife, Hannah. What's your name?"

"Tara," she replied softly.

"How long have you been on the streets, Tara?"

"Three days. My parents kicked me out of the house."

Tara went on to explain that she was eighteen years old and was seven months pregnant. Her parents had forced her to choose between her family and her boyfriend, JJ. When she chose JJ, the father of her child, she was made to leave their home in a neighboring town about 30 minutes away. They had hitched a ride to our town.

"Is JJ around?" we asked.

"Yes, he's the next block over trying to get us enough money for a hotel room tonight."

I walked down the street and found JJ at the next light and asked him to come with me.

I offered to get them off the street for the night if they wanted our help. They readily agreed.

My wife took our kids home and I took JJ and Tara to get some food at a local drive-thru and then to a discount department store to get some clean clothes. Then, I drove them to a hotel nearby and booked them for a one-night stay with the promise that I would be back in the morning to pick them up and take them to get more long-term help and support.

I drove home that night convinced that I had now done all that God required. Tomorrow, I would get them into a local homeless shelter and my work here would be complete. I had done the will of God.

But little did I know, the work was only just beginning.

The Will of God

What is the will of God? When I was in my twenties and thirties, I wrestled with this question a lot. I was convinced that the will of God was a very specific path laid out for me and I worried that I would somehow miss it. That I would choose wrongly when it came to career, family, or finances and therefore be outside of God's will.

But then one day, I read these words in 1 Peter 2:21:

"For God called you to do good, even if it means suffering. Just as Christ suffered for you. He is your example, and you must follow in His steps."

The will of God is not about what you do, but about who you'll become.

God has called us to do good by following the example of Jesus.

God's will is not a cosmic set of turn-by-turn directions for our lives. It's an orientation toward the goodness embodied in His son.

The decision to come to faith is often described to children (and sometimes adults too) as needing to ask Jesus into our hearts—and as I was growing up in Sunday School, that's what I believed.

But Jesus does not live in our hearts. No, Scripture tells us that Christ is seated at the right hand of the Father in heaven.

But my objection is more than just one of semantics. When I view my faith through a lens that I must ask Jesus into my heart, I make Jesus a character in the story of me.

This is *my* life. My faith. My story. And Jesus is one of the characters, perhaps even a main character, but it's still the story of me.

No, the Bible doesn't teach us to ask Jesus into our hearts, but rather it instructs us to follow, abide, and enter into Christ.

When I enter into Christ, I become a character in the story of Jesus.[23]

And His story always has a richer substance and the better ending. The stories we write for ourselves just aren't that good. Let's not limit Jesus to a character in your own story. Become a character in the story of Jesus.

Playing Our Part

If we are to be a character in the story of Jesus, what is the part we are to play?

1 Peter 2:9 describes it this way: "For you are a chosen people. You are royal priests, a holy nation, God's very own possession. As a result, you can show others the goodness of God, for he called you out of the darkness into his wonderful light."

---

[23] Thanks to Pastor Derek Vreeland for seeding this thinking during a conversation over Zoom years ago.

In reminding followers of Jesus that they are a chosen people and a royal priesthood, Peter is pointing them to their original vocation as God's image-bearers. The nation of Israel was not chosen because they were better or more special to God than other peoples. They were called a chosen people because God chose them to be his image-bearers on the earth, a people who would reflect God's love and character to the rest of the world.

A priest had two primary responsibilities – worship and witness. They were to worship God and to bear witness to humanity about God. The same calling exists for us as followers of Jesus today.

If the foundation of our faith is asking Jesus into our heart and inviting him into *our* story, then the goal of the Christian life is reduced to going to heaven. But if the foundation of our faith is that we abide in Christ and enter into *His* story, then the goal of our Christian life is the redeeming of the world.

To paraphrase N.T. Wright, God is not rescuing us so we can escape the world by going to heaven. God is rescuing us so we can escape death and cooperate with God in the work of redeeming the world.[24]

In his book, *The Day the Revolution Began*, Wright challenges a theological view that he calls the "works contract." In short, the works contract holds that God made human beings to follow the rules. The rules have been broken by sin and somebody must be punished. For the Christian then, Jesus takes our punishment upon himself. For those outside the faith, fire and brimstone await.

But Wright suggests that the grand story of Scripture doesn't describe a works contract, but rather a covenant of vocation, in which God created humanity in His image to reflect God's love into the world. Humanity has sinned by worshipping as God that which is not God and now reflects a broken image into the world.

---

[24] Derek Vreeland, "N.T. Wright and the Revolutionary Cross: Week 3," Derek Vreeland online, March 17, 2017, https://derekvreeland.com/2017/03/n-t-wright-revolutionary-cross-week-3/.

As a result, humanity needs to be transformed back into God's image-bearing creatures.

God's will for our lives is not simply punching our ticket to the afterlife, but to be transformed so that we may rightly bear His image and be a part of God's redemptive work in the world in which we live.

When I Grow Up

About the time that children enter kindergarten, adults begin asking them that age-old question: "What do you want to be when you grow up?" It's cute when their young because they usually have the same pat answers – a police officer, a doctor, a veterinarian, or a professional athlete. My favorite answer was the little kid who told me he wanted to be a hip-hop dancer when he grew up. You go, boy.

Here's the problem with this question in the 21st century. The US Department of Labor estimates that 65% of today's students will do jobs in the future that do not yet exist.[25] Nearly two-thirds of the students sitting in our K-12 schools right now will do jobs we can't even yet describe. So when kids and teens are asked what they want to be when they grow up, more than half couldn't answer correctly even if they wanted to.

The question is no longer, "What do you want to be?" The better question to ask is what problem do you want to solve? What new thing do you want to create?

In Genesis 1:28, what is sometimes called the Creation Mandate, we find guidance to help us answer these questions.

Then God blessed them, and God said to them, "Be fruitful and multiply; fill the earth and subdue it; have dominion

---

25 "The Future of Jobs," World Economic Forum online, January 18, 2016, https://reports.weforum.org/future-of-jobs-2016/chapter-1-the-future-of-jobs-and-skills/.

over the fish of the sea, over the birds of the air, and over every living thing that moves on the earth. (NKJV)

In his book *Faith for Exiles: 5 Ways for a New Generation to Follow Jesus in Digital Babylon*, David Kinnaman summarizes the three things God designed work to do: create beauty, create order, and create abundance.[26]

Creating Beauty

In the beginning, God created. But He didn't just create a world that worked. He also fashioned it in a way that displayed great beauty. God is not a pragmatist, concerned only with function. He is an artist who elevates the aesthetic.

Some of us, as God's image-bearers, are also called to create beauty. These are the creatives among us. The ones who pen stories and poems, make art, sing songs, record films, and choreograph dance. We need creatives in our world because they have the prophetic imaginations to reminds us of what is possible. When we become content with the world as it is and begin to accept the brokenness around us as "normal," it is the creatives – our modern-day prophets – who call us to envision something better. As Pastor Brian Zahnd once quipped, "When God wanted to get the attention of his people, He didn't send politicians to write policies, He sent prophets to write poetry."

One of my favorite movies is *Remember the Titans*. If I'm channel-surfing and that movie is on, I will stop and watch it no matter how many times I have seen it. I love it because amid racial unrest, it offers an aspirational vision of how things can be. That's the power of creating beauty. It can reorient our imaginations.

---

[26] David Kinnaman, *Faith for Exiles: 5 Ways for a New Generation to Follow Jesus in Digital Babylon* (Ada: Baker Books, 2019).

Creating Abundance

In God's mandate to creation, He instructed humanity to "be fruitful and multiply."

The second God-given calling is to create abundance. This calling is manifested in those with an entrepreneurial gifting. These individuals have a natural ability to help things grow, whether in finances, leadership, or organizations. Despite the vast abundance of resources in our world, much of humanity lives with a scarcity mindset, believing that there is not enough for everyone. We need those who can create abundance – not for personal wealth or gain – but to meet the needs of those without.

I remember visiting the slums of Nairobi, Kenya, on the day that one of America's billionaires made his first trip into outer space. Looking up into the heavens from the heart of Mukuru, a community with 300,000 people living on less than 700 acres, with no running water, no sewage system, no garbage disposal, and sharing just 3800 pit latrines, I was struck by the irony of the moment, and I posted this on Twitter: "Humanity is best served when we invest in creating a live-able world for all, not just a leave-able world for the few."[27] It's more miraculous to escape the gravitational pull of poverty than that of the earth. Creating abundance should mean more for everyone.

---

[27] McKenzie, Jim. Twitter Post. July 13, 2021, 3:26 AM. https://twitter.com/jcmckenzie/status/1414848665492021248

Creating Order

Finally, God mandates us to "fill the earth and subdue it; have dominion… over every living thing that moves on the earth."

The third God-given calling is to create order. These are the scientists, engineers, mathematicians, researchers, and managers among us. In a world that feels like it is falling into chaos every day, those who create order provide the structures for humanity to flourish together.

I am convinced that there are really only two kinds of people in the world: those who fold their toilet paper and those who crumple it. The crumplers are the creatives who live by their own set of rules, are typically disorganized, and rarely on time for anything. Their toilet paper is probably not even on the holder, but set on top of it, or on the back of the toilet, or even just there on the floor next to the commode. The folders are the ones who create order – in the bathroom and in the rest of the world – by building systems that lead to efficiency, structure, and the well-being of society.

With today's technology and agricultural growth, we are capable of adequately feeding up to 10 billion people, yet 690 million people are undernourished and food insecure.[28] How is it that Elon Musk can put his Tesla in orbit around the planet, but we can't get excess food production to the people who need it? It's not that we lack the technological or transportation solutions to get it done. It's that we lack the determination. Those gifted to create order can use their calling to generate solutions that bring healing to the broken areas of our world.

---

[28] Malav Dave, "There is a Global Food Surplus So Why Are Millions of People Still Food Insecure," Million Meals Mission online, April 22, 2021, https://www. millionmealsmission.org/post/there-is-a-global-food-surplus-so-why-are-millions-of-people-still-food-insecure.

Sacred-Secular Divide

A 2014 study by the Barna Group found that nearly six out of ten adults said they want to make a difference in the world. Yet only 40% of practicing Christians say they have a clear sense of God's calling on their lives.[29] A majority of Christians and non-Christians alike want to do work that matters, but even within the Church, most Christians seem unclear about God's calling for their life and work. Why is there such confusion?

I believe it's rooted in what some have defined as the sacred-secular divide, a notion that suggests that there are some things that God cares deeply about (sacred) and other things that God is less concerned with (secular). Bryan Smith of Bob Jones University illustrates this dichotomy with a photo of a two-story building where the top floor is a church, and the bottom floor is a house. The ground floor represents the secular – things like math and science and career and government – where God is indifferent. The second story represents the sacred – things like ministry and missions and seminary and church work – that are at the very heart of God. Most of us live downstairs. God lives upstairs with His chosen few.

And even though we don't explicitly hold to this two-story view, we silently adopt this mindset when we narrowly define a calling as that of only full-time ministry work. The sacred-secular divide is a myth that seeks to limit what matters to God. In truth, "the earth is the Lord's, and everything in it. The world and all its people belong to him."[30]

All work is sacred because He cares about all of it and all of us.

---

[29] "Three Trends on Faith, Work, and Calling," Barna Group online, February 11, 2014, https://www.barna.com/research/three-trends-on-faith-work-and-calling/.

[30] Psalms 24:1

Whatcha Gonna Do About It?

In Matthew 6:33, we find these words from Jesus' Sermon on the Mount, "But seek first the kingdom of God and His righteousness, and all these things shall be added to you." (NKJV)

This is one of those verses that I refer to as Coffee Cup Christianity. It's verses like Matthew 6:33, Jeremiah 29:11, and other popular and likable scriptures we print on coffee cups and refrigerator magnets. We name-it-claim-it-frame-it all while missing the real meaning embedded in the context of the surrounding passage.

In Matthew 6:33, what we believe Jesus said was, "Live a moral life and God will reward you."

But a closer examination of the word that we translate as righteousness provides a richer context. The Greek word is *dikaiosyne* and it has two translations – righteousness and justice.

Righteousness can be defined as setting things right in our relationship with God.

Justice can be defined as setting things right in the wider world in which we live.

In the English language, we use two different words, but in the Greek, there is only one word, *dikaiosyne*. In this way, we can read righteousness as simultaneously setting things right with both God and our world.

In this light, I think a more accurate understanding of Jesus' command in Matthew 6:33 would be this: "Make it your priority to bring heaven to earth by establishing God's justice here and now and God will provide everything you need to do it."

Growing up in the days before the internet and social media, the school bully was the big kid who liked to pick on the little kids, steal his lunch money, or knock his books out of his hands. And to flaunt his status as the bully, he always made the same remark after his abusive behavior. He'd look down upon his victim and say, "Whatcha gonna do about it?" It was a smug remark inviting retaliation while also letting everyone know the answer. Nothing. Nothing was going to be done about it.

Like a schoolyard bully, I believe the powers of darkness that wreak havoc in our world today are staring down the church and asking, "Whatcha gonna do about it?"

884 million people lack access to safe water.

840,000 people die each year worldwide from water-related disease.

Whatcha gonna do about it?

45 million people live in slavery worldwide.

5 million people worldwide will die of malnutrition.

Nearly 900,000 pregnancies are terminated in the United States each year.

Whatcha gonna do about it?

The problems are not just on a global scale. Your local community is facing challenges too. They may be related to homelessness, poverty, healthcare access, racial relations, educational equity, or environmental concerns. Again, whatcha gonna do about it?

Paul told the church in Rome, "Don't let evil conquer you, but conquer evil by doing good."[31]

I believe that God is calling each of us to do something.

At The Rock School, our students are invited to lead a Do Something Project. This is an opportunity for them to propose a project to solve a problem in our local community or broader global

---

[31] Romans 12:21

context. In doing so, the school and our community come alongside to support them in their work. Over the years, students from eight to eighteen organized projects to purchase new shoes for foster children, collect coats and blankets for those in local homeless shelters, clean up coastal waterways, and raise funds to dig wells in third-world countries.

Whatcha gonna do about it?

One-Way Missionaries

In his book, *All In*, Mark Batterson tells the story of a group from the early 20th century who became known as one-way missionaries.[32] It was said that they purchased one-way tickets to their destinations and that they packed their belongings in a casket instead of a suitcase. They knew that they would never return home.

One such missionary was A.W. Milne who traveled to an island in the South Pacific inhabited by headhunters who had martyred the missionaries who had gone before him. But Milne made his way there and lived among the people for thirty-five years. When he died, the villagers inscribed upon his tombstone:

When he came there was no light.
When he left there was no darkness.

Whatcha gonna do about it? Milne's answer was clear and emphatic: I will do something.

---

[32] Mark Batterson, *All In: You Are One Decision Away from a Totally Different Life* (Grand Rapids: Zondervan, 2013).

Living as Exiles

The nation of Israel was taken captive by the Babylonians in 587 B.C. They were uprooted from their homeland and forced to travel 700 miles to a foreign land. The people complained about their new circumstances and wallowed in self-pity. The prophets Ahab, Zedekiah, and Shemiah stoked their discontent and promised that God would soon deliver them from exile. The message was simple: "Just hang in there a little longer, it will be over soon."

But then one day, two messengers arrive in Babylon from Jerusalem, bearing a letter from the prophet Jeremiah. It was a word to the exiles:

"This is what the Lord of Heaven's Armies, the God of Israel, says to all the captives he has exiled to Babylon from Jerusalem: "Build homes, and plan to stay. Plant gardens and eat the food they produce. Marry and have children. Then find spouses for them so that you may have many grandchildren. Multiply! Do not dwindle away! And work for the peace and prosperity of the city where I sent you into exile. Pray to the Lord for it, for its welfare will determine your welfare."

This is what the Lord of Heaven's Armies, the God of Israel, says: "Do not let your prophets and fortune-tellers who are with you in the land of Babylon trick you. Do not listen to their dreams, because they are telling you lies in my name. I have not sent them," says the Lord. This is what the Lord says: "You will be in Babylon for seventy years. But then I will come and do for you all the good things I have promised, and I will bring you home again. For I know the plans

I have for you," says the Lord. "They are plans for good and not for disaster, to give you a future and a hope."[33]

Jeremiah instructs the exiles to stop sitting idly by and waiting for rescue. The prophets are wrong, God's deliverance will not come soon. He challenges the Israelites to engage with the culture in which they now reside, to build homes and plant gardens. To carry on with life, to marry and procreate.

And then in verse 7, the Lord says for them to "work for the peace and prosperity of the city… for its welfare will determine your welfare." The Hebrew word translated as welfare here is *shalom*. As we saw in Chapter One, shalom is about flourishing. Thus, Jeremiah's letter encourages the exiled peoples to seek the flourishing of their city of exile, because when the city flourishes, they will flourish too.

Living as exiles, we are to work toward the flourishing of our cities. We should not live as isolationists who withdraw from culture, nor should we live as combatants who want to war with our culture. Instead, let us seek the peace and prosperity of the communities where we live.

Jeremiah 29:11 (another coffee cup verse) is not a guarantee of some bright and prosperous feel-good future for Christians, but rather a promise that God has not forgotten us in our exile and is working things out for our good as we seek the shalom of our neighbors and neighborhoods.

> "For I know the plans I have for you," says the Lord. "They are plans for good and not for disaster, to give you a future and a hope."

---

[33] Jeremiah 29:4-11

Jesus and Justice

As Skye Jethani notes, for too long the Church "has struggled to reconcile the call to individual reconciliation with God (evangelism) with the call to social reconciliation between people (justice)."[34] The American Church continues to argue over the proper order for evangelism and justice while we slide further into cultural irrelevance.

Jesus without justice is unloving. To preach a Gospel that offers heaven in the future without also addressing the hell of the present day is just not love.

So too, justice without Jesus is unloving. Without the forgiving message of the Gospel, the work of justice is driven by vengeance. Rather than working to set things right, we work to punish those who are wrong.

Yale theologian Miroslav Volf posted this on Twitter in 2020: "Let's not play personal and systemic sins – racism, e.g. – against each other! Sin is embedded in shared practices, public institutions, and cultural moods and it occupies and poisons individual hearts. Sin within echoes the sin without; sin without is enlivened by the sin within."[35]

If we believe in human depravity and that we are born with a sinful nature, then we must acknowledge that a sinful people working together creates sinful systems. And while the individuals may eventually be redeemed of their sinful ways, the systems they created remain unchanged. Thus, it remains the work of the Church to both redeem the individual's sins (evangelism) while also working to redeem the culture's systemic sins (justice).

We don't lead with evangelism or with justice; we lead with love. Evangelism and justice are the expression of that love to the world.

---

[34] Skye Jethani, *What If Jesus Was Serious?* (Chicago: Moody Publishers, 2020), pp. 46.

[35] Volf, Miroslav. Twitter Post. June 14, 2020, 3:04 PM. https://twitter.com/miroslavvolf/status/1272243550919458816

How do we respond to injustice? I see three ways that people generally react to the injustices around them.

1. Apathy – Apathy is generally revealed in language that suggests, "I don't care" or "It's not my problem." The apathetic response is an unloving approach to a broken world because it lacks empathy or compassion for others. It dismisses the need for justice as a relatively unimportant pursuit.

2. Acceptance – Acceptance is manifested in statements like, "It is what it is" or "they probably deserve it." The accepting response is an unloving approach because it suggests a lack of faith in God. It becomes a solemn resignation that there is no hope this side of eternity, and we must learn to live with the brokenness.

3. Action – Action can be observed in affirming language such as, "It doesn't have to be this way" or "I can help!" Unlike apathy and acceptance, action reflects a loving response because it acknowledges the brokenness and commits to do something. Rather than dismissal or resignation, action is fueled by a faith that God is at work in the world, and He is making all things new. We don't have to sit idly and wait; we can cooperate with Him in the work of redeeming the world.

Do Something

It was time to pick up JJ and Tara from the hotel and take them to the local homeless shelter. There was just one problem. When I called to make the arrangements for their stay, I was told the shelter was full and had a long waiting list. I called two other organizations that work with the homeless population. They were also full.

I had no choice but to put them up in the hotel for the weekend, so I walked to the hotel registry and asked to extend the reservation for another two nights. There were no rooms available. The hometown college football team had a home game, and all the hotels were sold out for the weekend.

After an hour on the phone, I finally found a place for them to stay. And so began a three-month journey to help JJ and Tara to get IDs, jobs, prenatal care, and housing. I spent hours and hours each week working through one obstacle after the next, calling every person in my contact list to advocate for the two of them.

By November, they had gainful employment and an apartment of their own. They spent Thanksgiving and Christmas with our family. They wanted to get married, so we arranged for a small but beautiful wedding for them. And in early January, Tara gave birth to her son, Jamie, and we were among the first to meet him.

It seemed like the fairytale ending. But unfortunately, it didn't turn out that way.

Six months later, Tara and JJ were struggling. JJ was becoming verbally abusive. Neither were working. They'd lost their housing and were staying with some people they had met not long ago. And now they were using drugs, and someone had reported them to child services.

We had just returned from a day at the beach when we got the call. Would we take baby Jamie in as foster parents to keep him out of the official foster care system. We said yes.

For the next eight months, Jamie was in and out of our home. We cared for him like he was our own until the day he left us for good. Mom and dad eventually split up, but Jamie was reunited with Tara. Our relationship with Tara became tenuous during our fostering season as she blamed us for not being able to get her son back.

I think back often to the first time I met Tara and those words that God spoke to my heart, "You can do better." I don't regret the decision to help. I don't consider the time and money invested to have been in vain. It didn't have a happily-ever-after kind of ending, but I know that I obeyed God. The rest I leave to Him.

You see, I believe that God's solution to the widespread injustice and the deep brokenness of our world is you and me.

We can all do better.

What is God calling you to do?

Do something.

CHAPTER FIVE

Stand Watch

A five-foot water moccasin and a five-year-old boy are on a collision course in the swimming area of a neighborhood lake. I am chasing the snake, waiting for the right moment to grab it by the tail, sling it out of the way, and hope to God I don't get bit.

I'm afraid of snakes. No, that's putting it too mildly. I am terrified of snakes. Friends remind me that I only need to be worried about the venomous ones, but I don't ever want to be close enough to a snake to know the difference.

When I found a snake coiled up under the seat of my riding lawn mower, my wife—the nature lover—reassured me that it was just a friendly red rat snake. I don't care. If that thing had crawled out onto my lap while I was mowing, I would have had a heart attack, fallen off the mower, been chopped into pieces by the blades, and then eaten by the rat snake, friendly or not.

My fear of snakes goes all the way back to my childhood. As a kid, we raised rabbits on the back of the property beyond the garden. It was my job to feed the rabbits, but because I was so sure there were snakes in the garden, I was too afraid to walk to the rabbit pen to feed them. They all died.

When I was fourteen, I was camping with some friends. I had just lay down in my tent for the night when someone yelled, "Look at the size of this snake I caught." I was so relieved that I was cuddled inside my sleeping bag and not out there to see it. And then I heard the zipper on my tent open as someone yelled, "This is for you!" They tossed the snake on top of my sleeping bag. Screaming and thrashing, adrenaline pumping, I nearly tore the tent down trying to get out. "Get that thing out of my tent," I yelled at my friends, who stood around laughing hysterically. "I mean it!" I demanded. "Get it out now!" A moment later, one of the boys emerged holding a four-foot piece of garden hose they'd found down by the bath house.

And then there was that time, at seventeen, when a cottonmouth fell in my canoe because I slammed into some low-hanging branches while racing my friends and paddling way too fast for the tight and winding stream.

And yet, despite all my fears, here I am, running after, and not away from, my worst nightmare – a large, nasty, and venomous water moccasin. Why? Because, for better or worse, I am the lifeguard on duty.

Save Me, Lord

In Matthew 14:22-33, we read the account of Jesus as he walks on the water out to his disciples on their boat. At first, they are frightened for they think Jesus is a ghost, but Jesus offers reassuring words: "Don't be afraid. I am here."

> Then Peter called to him, "Lord, if it's really you, tell me to come to you, walking on the water."

"Yes, come," Jesus said. So Peter went over the side of the boat and walked on the water toward Jesus. But when he saw the strong wind and the waves, he was terrified and began to sink. "Save me, Lord!" he shouted. Jesus immediately reached out and grabbed him. "You have so little faith," Jesus said. "Why did you doubt me?"

We read this story and we marvel at the miracle that is Peter walking on water. What an amazing moment that must have been for him. With each step, Peter must be thinking, "Wow, I can't believe I'm really doing this! This is so cool!" The disciples watching must have been equally amazed.

But then Peter begins to see the wind and the waves and the stormy parts of the sea, and he becomes fearful, and suddenly he finds himself beginning to sink. In that moment of crisis, he cries out, "Save me, Lord!"

This is where pastors and preachers usually focus as the lesson from this story. On Peter. How he set his sights on his circumstances and not his savior and began to lose faith in both. And these are valuable lessons for us indeed.

But I want to consider the story from the other viewpoint, to see it from the eyes of Jesus and not Peter. I want us to examine how Jesus responded to Peter when Peter was in trouble.

Matthew records Peter's fearful words as he begins to sink: "Save me, Lord!" In that moment, Scripture tells us, "Jesus immediately reached out and grabbed him." Jesus wasn't going to let Peter drown.

And he won't let you drown either. You are going to be invited by God to take those leaps of faith, to step out of the boat, to walk on the water, to do the hard things, and to take some risks. When you find yourself in over your head, call out to Jesus, and let him reach out his hand and catch you.

But I also believe that we are to be the hands and feet of Jesus for others. Whether friends or family, colleagues or co-workers, roommates or residence hall neighbors, we can let them know that we are standing watch. There is a lifeguard on duty.

Lifeguard on Duty

When I was fifteen years old, I completed all the training to become a certified lifeguard by the American Red Cross. In high school and college, I worked each spring and summer as a lifeguard. I lived in North Central Florida, so most of my lifeguard work was at one of the local springs in the Ocala National Forest. But I also lived right down the road from a large church camp. This camp had a large swimming pool, and each week, different church groups would rent the venue to bring the children or youth from their congregations to spend a week at camp. To use the pool on the premises, the owners of the camp required each group to provide a certified lifeguard. Since most groups didn't know a freelance lifeguard, the camp staff would provide my contact information to the renters who would usually reach out to book me for their week.

I loved being a lifeguard. I'd spend the day working, then suit up and snorkel or scuba dive the springs after work. When I worked the pool, I got to meet new groups of people from around the state each week. I made a lot of new friends along the way. Oh, and the pay was pretty good, too.

When I was eighteen, I became a certified instructor to teach the Red Cross's Water Safety, Lifeguard, and First Aid & CPR courses. That season of life was very instructive, and I believe it helped point me toward my eventual vocation in education. But there are also things that I learned through those experiences on the water that have helped me understand how to be a lifeguard for people, not just at the pool, but in all of life.[36]

Training & Preparation

Like all first responders, lifeguards train so that they are properly prepared to respond in a time of need. Lifeguard training requires a demonstration of both physical competencies and academic competencies.

There's a physical training required of lifeguards. A lifeguard must be a strong swimmer with a high level of endurance in the water, both for their own safety, but also for the benefit of those that may need to be rescued. One of the most challenging tasks of the certification course was the swim test. One of the swim test requirements required candidates to tread water for three minutes while holding a ten-pound brick above the water. Because both hands are holding the brick, this exercise required swimmers to tread water in place using only their legs. I had perfected an egg-beater kind of kick where my legs moved in small alternating circles, so this test was easy for me. Some days I would tread water with the brick for ten minutes or more just for practice.

But for those who couldn't figure out the right leg kick, this was such a hard task. There were times I thought the trainee was at risk of drowning as we watched him exert so much energy kicking and splashing to barely hold the brick – and his head – above water. That was the make-or-break moment in the course for most people. After that, the swim requirements and the technical rescue skills came easy.

---

[36] Full disclosure: It's been 30 years since I worked as a lifeguard or trained others to do so. The information I share in this chapter about my training is from distant memories and is not likely an accurate description of current practices for lifeguards today. It should not be followed as advice for any actual water rescues.

What I didn't expect when I enrolled in the lifeguard course was all the academic content that was also required. In addition to the swim test, there is also an extensive written test. Lifeguards must be knowledgeable about rip currents and PH levels and supervisory techniques.

Together, the physical training and the classroom knowledge would combine for the skills assessment where each person would be required to make an appropriate rescue based on the various scenarios and how to use the right equipment properly in the process.

During those years, I would often get asked if I ever had to save someone? The answer to that is both yes and no. In all my years working as a lifeguard in an official capacity, I never had to make any serious rescues. On occasion, I would have to grab a kid who was struggling a little bit and guide her to the side of the pool or go help him from the deeper waters at the springs. But nothing immediately life-threatening.

The most serious rescue I was ever involved with happened at a time when I was not even working as a lifeguard. It was late December, and my best friend and I were in Crystal River, a small town on the west coast situated along a springs-fed river inhabited by manatees from the Gulf of Mexico during the winter months. It was our tradition to go there and swim with the manatees on the day after Christmas each year. (The water in springs remains a constant 72 degrees year-round, so it is possible to swim in December in Florida. It's only cold when you get out of the water!)

We had just returned to the small marina in our rented johnboat and were unloading our snorkeling gear when another boat came racing up to the dock. There was a woman lying on the floor of the boat. She was soaking wet and unconscious. She had drowned before being pulled into the boat. Once they got her onto the dock, we assisted with CPR until the paramedics arrived. I don't know what happened to her after that.

The most serious rescue I've ever been involved in happened at a time when I wasn't on duty. And it reminds me of what the apostle Paul wrote to young Timothy: "Preach the word of God. Be prepared, whether the time is favorable or not."[37]

In that moment at the dock, I was ready. My training had prepared me.

As Christians, there's a preparation and readiness that needs to take place in our lives too. Our fitness matters, physically, emotionally, and spiritually. This why Paul also instructed Timothy in his first letter to him:

Do not waste time arguing over godless ideas and old wives' tales. Instead, train yourself to be godly. "Physical training is good, but training for godliness is much better, promising benefits in this life and in the life to come." This is a trustworthy saying, and everyone should accept it. This is why we work hard and continue to struggle, for our hope is in the living God, who is the Savior of all people and particularly of all believers. Teach these things and insist that everyone learn them. Don't let anyone think less of you because you are young. Be an example to all believers in what you say, in the way you live, in your love, your faith, and your purity. Until I get there, focus on reading the Scriptures to the church, encouraging the believers, and teaching them.[38]

To be a lifeguard – to stand watch – means training for godliness so that we can be an example to others in our faith and love and life.

---

[37] I Timothy 4:2

[38] I Tim 4:7-13

A Safe Distance

Early in the training regimen, prospective lifeguards are reminded about personal safety. A hero complex can get you killed. Lifeguards are taught to keep a safe distance, but still reach out.

If you've ever watched a television show or a movie where a lifeguard scenario plays out, it's almost always done wrong. (I'm looking at you, *Baywatch*.) What we typically see is a lifeguard running down the beach in slow motion as the dramatic music builds, his tanned skin glistening, her sun-kissed hair blowing in the ocean breeze. Then, they dive into the ocean, swim out to the struggling swimmers, throw them on their hip, and bravely swim them to the shore. If the person is unconscious, they immediately proceed to do CPR – also very incorrectly – but I'll let that go for now.

It all makes for wonderful television drama, but, in the real world, it's an example of all the things they teach you not to do in an actual rescue scenario.

Every year, there are numerous reports of people attempting to aid a drowning victim only to drown themselves. It's so common, there's an official name for it – Aquatic Victim Instead of Rescuer (AVIR) syndrome.[39]

One study from Australia found that during a five-year period, 17 rescuers drowned in 15 incidents involving a drowning child. Ironically, 93% of the children survived, while the rescuers did not.[40]

Drowning victims, even children and especially adults, are dangerous. A panicked person will exhibit enormous strength aided

---

[39] Esther Ingles-Arkell, "Why Rescuers Die While Drowning Victims Survive," Gizmodo online, January 19, 2015, https://gizmodo.com/why-rescuers-die-while-drowning-victims-survive-1680233920.

[40] Richard C. Franklin, "Drowning for love: the aquatic victim-instead-of-rescuer syndrome: drowning fatalities involving those attempting to rescue a child," Pub Med online, October 26, 2010, https://pubmed.ncbi.nlm.nih.gov/20973865/.

by a surge of adrenaline and desperation. They will instinctively grab onto and even climb on top of another person – pushing them below the surface in the process – all to keep their own head above water.

They will put you down to remain on top.

As such, even professionally trained lifeguards are instructed, whenever possible, to avoid contact with a drowning victim. Instead, they are taught to use rescue cans, tubes, or ring buoys. This equipment allows the lifeguard to maintain a safe boundary between the victim and the rescuer.

I've had to make a rescue (in drills only, thankfully) of another adult without the aid of flotation devices, and it was terrifying. In my first attempt, I swam up to the instructor (a very fit 200-pound man who played the role of a drowning victim). I offered reassuring words that I was there to help him when he suddenly lunged at me and grabbed my arms. Before I even realized what was happening, he had pulled into his body, wrapped his arms around me, pushed me under the surface, and was sitting on my shoulders, his legs locked around my neck. In real life, I would have drowned thirty seconds later after exhausting all my oxygen and energy in a desperate but futile attempt to escape his grasp before an involuntary gasp of water filled my lungs. The news would have reported two deaths, one from drowning, and the other from AVIR syndrome.

I learned an important lesson that day. When someone is drowning, don't engage. Keep a safe distance. It's good to help those in need, but my safety matters too.

If you have people in your life who are drowning, offer help, but remember that your personal wellness is important too. Maintain healthy boundaries. Don't become another rescuer-turned-AVIR.

When double drownings occur, no one ever blames the original drowning victim. And why should we? They behave exactly as one would expect from those who are drowning and fearful for their lives. They'll put others down to remain on top.

In the same way, we should not be so surprised when hurt people behave in hurtful ways toward us and others. The people in your life who put you down – either in word or deed – they are drowning.

Hurt people hurt people. Healthy people heal.

If you have been hurt by someone else, whether past or present, I need you to understand that it is not about you. It is about them. When someone mistreats you or wrongs you in some way, it says nothing about you. But it says everything about them.

They are drowning and they're doing exactly what drowning people do, desperately pushing others down to try to stay afloat. Yes, it's a completely irrational response. In his right mind, a drowning victim would see a rescuer coming and calmly cooperate in order that they both might return safely to shore. But the fight-or-flight response tells a different story.

When you aim to help those closest to you during their challenging seasons and they respond to you in irrational and hurtful ways, remember this: it's not personal. Hurt people hurt people. In those moments, keep a safe distance. Don't get pulled into the drama of another and sacrifice your own well-being. If you're struggling to stay afloat, stop helping. Don't let them drown you too.

Going Under

As we've seen, engaging with a drowning person is dangerous, and even well-intentioned efforts to help can escalate into greater conflict. But what if someone is drowning and the rescuer doesn't have a flotation device to use? What if keeping a safe distance means letting the person drown? When faced with conflict on the surface, lifeguards go under.

To make a safe rescue when direct physical contact with the drowning victim is required, I was taught to go under.[41] If I try to make a rescue at the surface, I'm likely to end up in a wrestling match that could easily end with me in a headlock under the water as I discovered in that first simulated rescue of my instructor. We could both end up drowning. Rather than engaging at the surface, as I approached the struggling swimmer, I would instead dive down under the water, and swim underneath him. Then, I would grab his feet and pull down hard, forcing him under. The natural reaction when people are pulled underwater is for their hands to shoot up over their heads. In this position, where their entire body is in one long line as if they were stretching upward from their toes to fingers, they can be more easily subdued. In this moment, I would grab him from behind across his chest and under his armpit, squeezing as hard as necessary to maintain control, and surface with his lower back supported by my hip, swimming sideways safely back to shore.

When we see someone drowning in life, we can take the same approach. Instead of engaging in the conflict and allowing it to escalate and risk the well-being of everyone involved, we can simply choose to go under. We choose humility.

Lifeguards make rescues from a position of strength and readiness, not from a place of deep hurt. Going under does not mean enduring abuse for the sake of another. Your physical, mental, and spiritual safety matters too.

Going under means that instead of standing our ground, that we humble ourselves to do what is necessary to bring peace and resolution in the relationship. Our natural tendency is to argue and fight and push back and to engage in conflict. We choose to trade words, trade punches, and trade text messages. And yet the best thing to do is to go under. It is to choose a position of humility. If we are to be lifeguards, if we are to bring healing to broken relationships, if

---

[41] Full disclosure: I did not learn this in my lifeguard course, but from an unaffiliated water safety instructor.

we are to aid someone who is drowning, then a show of humility is better than a show of strength.

Sometimes it's better to do right than to be right. Assuming a posture of humility – going under – leads us and others to shalom. Remember, drowning people behave like drowning people. They will not willingly go under, but you can.

Paul encouraged the church at Philippi on this matter when he wrote, "Don't be selfish; don't try to impress others. Be humble, thinking of others as better than yourselves. Don't look out only for your own interests, but take an interest in others, too."[42]

Stabilize the Broken

The most challenging rescue as a lifeguard is not pulling a panicked 200-pound man out of the ocean, as difficult and dangerous as that is. No, the hardest rescue to make is the one involving an unconscious victim floating face-down in a swimming pool. Ironically, the fact that they are unresponsive makes this more difficult than an active drowning scenario. When we observe someone floating face down in a swimming pool, the natural response would likely be to jump into the water, pull them to the side of the pool, and get them out of the water as quickly as possible and began rescue breathing or CPR. But, in this situation, we must assume the possibility that the person dove into the shallow end and suffered a serious head or neck injury. If this is true, then jumping in the water and creating waves, or grabbing, pulling, or rolling the victim over, could worsen a neck or spinal injury. Instead, lifeguards slip into the pool to avoid making waves. They approach the situation cautiously, not aggressively. Upon reaching the victim, they use a stabilizing technique in which they place one arm along the spine using the hand to hold

---

[42] Philippians 2:3-4

the neck while placing the other arm along the sternum and using that hand to secure the head, bracing the chin between the thumb and fingers. Squeezing their arms together to stabilize the spine and neck, they take a breath and slowly turn the victim over by rolling under them in the water. From this position in the water, a lifeguard can administer rescue breaths while keeping the spine stabilized until paramedics arrive. If CPR is needed, the victim can be placed on a rescue board in the water and lifted out of the pool. The key to a successful rescue begins with a gentle response.

When people hit rock bottom, it can break them. So often, our reaction to broken people is forceful and aggressive, when what is needed, is a gentle and measured response. Our instincts might prompt us to go full hero-mode but stabilizing the broken requires tenderness and grace.

We see this in Jesus' response to Peter as he was sinking amongst the waves. Jesus reached out his hand and pulled Peter to safety. Only then did Jesus say to Peter, "You have so little faith. Why did you doubt me?" Jesus brought stability first, and correction second. He made sure Peter felt safe before he corrected him.

A lifeguard doesn't chastise the victim floating unconscious in the water by pointing at the sign that says, "No Diving Allowed." He seeks to stabilize the broken. Too often, our default when we encounter others amid their adversity, rather than pulling them to safety, we choose to dish out a whole bunch of advice. We want to explain to them why we think they're in their current predicament. But whether they're drowning in water or in life, they suffer the real consequences of their actions. This is what Paul described when he wrote that "the wages of sin is death."[43]

Do we need correction? Absolutely. But we'll seldom be able to receive it thoughtfully until we know that we are safe. Let's follow the example of Jesus and offer a helping hand before a corrective word.

---

[43] Romans 6:23

Watch and Warn

Lifeguards strive for prevention rather than intervention. The goal of every lifeguard is not to make successful rescues, but to create a safe environment so that rescues are not necessary. To that end, they watch, and they warn.

Much of my work as a lifeguard was simply blowing my whistle and issuing a warning. When I was at a pool, it was usually to tell kids to stop running around by the water's edge or doing backflips into the shallow end. But because I often worked at springs and lakes in Florida, there were three things that required watching and warning: lightning, alligators, and snakes.

Florida summers bring consistent thunderstorms most afternoons. I would have to monitor the sky for lightning and at the first visible strike or audible thunder, I had to blow my whistle and instruct everyone to exit the water. People didn't like that, and I often had to repeat my instructions forcefully to get everyone to comply. I faced plenty of criticism, but it was my responsibility to ensure everyone's safety. On those occasions when an alligator or water snake entered the swimming area, the guests were much more cooperative in exiting the water on my whistle. Apparently, the swimmers feared a gator's bite more than a lightning bolt.

When I was on duty, I would alternate between walking back and forth along the water's edge and sitting up in the lifeguard tower. Near the water's edge, I had opportunity to connect with the park's guests and give casual safety reminders to individuals without needing to blow my whistle and draw everyone's attention. Sitting up in the lifeguard tower gave me a better vantage point of what was happening on the beach and in the water. It was great to be down among the people, but it didn't offer a complete view. I needed to ascend to a higher place to gain a proper perspective from which to watch and warn.

To watch and warn was the work of the Old Testament prophets too. God instructed Ezekiel, saying,

> Son of man, I have appointed you as a watchman for Israel. Whenever you receive a message from me, warn people immediately. If I warn the wicked, saying, 'You are under the penalty of death,' but you fail to deliver the warning, they will die in their sins. And I will hold you responsible for their deaths. If you warn them and they refuse to repent and keep on sinning, they will die in their sins. But you will have saved yourself because you obeyed me.

We are commissioned by God to be watchmen. We have a responsibility to watch and warn, so let us ascend to high places so that we can find a better view. When our feet touch the earth, we become mired in everything that's happening to us and around us and we don't see clearly. But when we ascend to a high place, when we stretch our hearts toward heaven and the one seated upon the throne, we gain the proper perspective.

If our only vantage point for viewing the world is through the lens of Instagram and TikTok and YouTube and Apple Music, we'll live with a distorted view of reality. Instead, let us pray and live out Jesus' bold decree, "May your Kingdom come soon. May your will be done on earth, as it is in heaven."[44]

There are two types of drowning victims. The first is the one we see splashing around in the water, frantically trying to keep her head above water. We've looked at the different ways to engage with her. But there are also those who just quietly slip under the surface and nobody even notices. We call this a silent drowning. I believe that we encounter both of these in the people around us every day. We have friends, siblings, classmates, and co-workers that are

---

[44] Matthew 6:10

drowning. Some of them are obvious and visible. They are open and honest with you about their lives. Or they're making such a scene that their cry for help can't go unnoticed. But there are also others that are silently drowning, and no one knows. They're too proud or too private or too afraid to cry out for help.

I woke up one morning during a Christmas break to an alert in my inbox. During the night, our school's filtering software had flagged a Google document in a sophomore's school account for language related to self-harm. This is not entirely uncommon and many times the algorithm flags words and statements that were used quite harmlessly. But this one was different. It was titled, "My Last Letter" and it was a long and detailed note that began, "I chose to end my life; to put it simply, there were days when I felt empty and broken. I felt stripped of my pride, with nothing left to give. I didn't want to endure my pain, so I left."

I called our school principal, and we immediately began trying to reach the family. We called the parents' home numbers, cell numbers, and work numbers. No answer. We tracked down the student's cell phone number and called. No response. We texted. No reply.

I looked up the family's address and jumped in my car. As I made the ten-minute drive to their home, I prayed desperately. "God, I don't know what I'm about to find, but please help me be your hands and feet and voice in this moment. Spirit, come!"

I pulled up to their home and knocked on the door. The little sister came to the door.

"Are your parents here?"

"Yes," she answered. "My daddy is home, but he's still in bed."

"Is your sister around?" I asked carefully.

"No, she's still in her room."

My heart sank and my voice cracked, "Oh, okay. Can you please go wake up your Daddy and tell him I need to speak with him?"

A few moments later the father emerged from his room and met me at the front door with a big smile and a firm handshake. "Good morning, Jim. How are you?" he asked with such enthusiasm.

As calmly as I could, I replied, "I need you to go check on your daughter right now. She wrote a very concerning letter late last night and I am worried about her."

I saw the flicker of fear in his eyes. I nodded, willing him to go.

As he turned to race upstairs, his daughter appeared from around the corner, holding her cell phone to her ear. She was alive! I could hear the principal's voice on the phone. The student had finally awakened and saw the text messages and called her back.

"I need you to go downstairs right now to see your father. He's with Mr. McKenzie at your front door," she ordered. "You need to show them that you are okay."

For the next twenty minutes, I stood in the driveway to explain to the father about the letter and our attempts to contact the family before driving over. He expressed his gratitude and his intention to take all the appropriate next steps.

As I pulled out of the driveway, I began to sob. The emotions of the morning and what could have been all came flooding out. I rejoiced that what looked like a tragic day was going to be okay. She was silently slipping under the water, but her small cry for help was enough for us to reach out and pull her to safety.

And so, we continue to watch and to warn.

Stay Alert

It was Peter, who Jesus pulled to safety years earlier, that wrote to the persecuted Christians living in Asia Minor in his first letter, "Stay alert! Watch out for your great enemy, the devil. He prowls around like a roaring lion, looking for someone to devour."[45]

I was the lifeguard on duty. I was watching when the water moccasin left the brush and entered the swimming area of the lake. I warned everyone to exit the water quickly. And yet, I am now chasing this terrifying creature in knee-deep water as he makes a direct line toward an unknowing five-year-old boy swimming toward it. It's large and venomous and its bite could prove deadly, given that the nearest hospital is at least twenty minutes away. I am splashing and yelling and doing everything I can to draw the snake's attention away, but now I have no choice. I am going to grab it by the tail and sling it. The sounds of the people around me have faded. I hear only the muffled sound of my heartbeat. I take a breath, steel my nerves, and lunge toward the tail.

But I missed.

At that exact moment, the snake made a sudden turn ninety degrees left and continued parallel to the shoreline until it exited the swimming area on the other side.

The enemy is always looking for someone to devour. Stay alert. Stand watch.

---

[45] 1 Peter 5:8

CHAPTER SIX

Start Small

When I was in eighth grade, I spent my entire Christmas Break writing an essay for English class. I was so proud of what I'd written and so excited to turn it into my teacher. But the day it was handed back with a big red F at the top was the day I swore I'd never write another word in my life.

By my third year in middle school, I had established myself as the math and science kid. A Science Fair winner and a MathCounts Champion. I could stand next to a skeleton and rattle off all the major bones in the body in less than 30 seconds. I could do Algebra and Geometry quickly and easily. I was even a voracious reader. But I did not like to write. At all. Maybe it's because I never learned cursive. (I still print in all-caps to this day.) Maybe it's because I'm left-handed and all those darn notebooks have the spiral on the wrong side and it gets in the way of my hand. Or maybe it was because I simply never knew what to write about.

Heading into Christmas Break, my Language Arts teacher assigned us an essay to write over the holidays. (Who does that to a middle school kid, by the way?) It was a prompt for an essay contest hosted by a local civic organization and it asked students to answer the question, "What does the Declaration of Independence mean to me?"

The contest required the teacher to pick two winners from my class to submit to the civic organization for consideration and the contest had a fifty-dollar prize for the top three essays from our area. For a kid who doesn't like to write, this was the perfect setup because it tapped into two things that I liked very much – competition and money.

So, over the break, I worked really hard on this essay, typing it page by page on my TRS-80 computer (Google it!). And the more that I wrote, the more I discovered how much I was enjoying writing. The night before school was to resume, I printed out my essay on my dot-matrix printer (Google it!) and excitedly went to bed, dreaming about the surprised look on my teacher's face when he would read my essay and thinking about all the ways I would spend the prize money.

A week later, the teacher announced that he was ready to hand back our essays. After he passed them all out, he would announce the names of the top two students whose essays had been selected for the area contest. I could hardly contain my excitement as he walked up and down the aisles passing out the papers. When he arrived at my seat, he placed it face-down on my desk with a blank expression on his face. How odd, I thought. I turned the paper over, and there at the top, was a big, bold, red F, and a note in pen below it: "This is clearly plagiarized. You are not capable of such quality of work."

Heartbroken and humiliated, I swore that day that I would never try to write again. I would stick to math and science and the things in my life that were positively reinforced. Why write? The experience was simply too painful.

Sometimes Big in Small Ways

One of my duties as a school administrator is I help students with the college admissions process. When students get to high school, my staff and I start talking to them about what they need to be doing to prepare themselves to make applications to the colleges of their choice in the fall of their senior year.

We talk about the importance of maintaining a good grade point average and preparing for the SAT and ACT college entrance exams. Colleges and universities generally try to take a holistic approach to evaluating students in the admissions process, so in addition to objective data points like GPA and test scores, they look at the level and rigor of the coursework that students complete. They weigh the honors and awards students earn and consider the extracurricular activities, community service, and leadership opportunities that students pursue. Many evaluate the student's writing skills through a personal essay. And usually, the final piece is to submit a letter of recommendation from someone who knows the student well-enough to attest to their college readiness. Ultimately, colleges and universities evaluate all these criteria to decide, is this student a candidate that we want to have in our school?

As I was guiding my students through this process year after year after year, I began to wonder, is there something more? On the surface, I think there is merit in these areas of evaluation. They speak to a student's achievements and work ethic, but all of it is rooted in performance. There is no room for consideration of character or virtue or passion.

If we're preparing our students for their future, what does God care about? What would be God's selection criteria? If God needed to decide who to appoint to lead the next generation, what would be most important to Him? I'm fairly certain that it's not anything found on a college application. I don't think he's concerned about our SATs, our GPAs, or the grammatical proficiency of our personal essays.

I believe that God's selection process is summarized in Paul's first letter to the church at Corinth, when he wrote in Chapter 1, verse 27: "Instead, God chose things the world considers foolish in order to shame those who think they are wise. And he chose things that are powerless to shame those who are powerful."

As we look throughout Scripture, we see this illustrated time and again. God used an orphan, Moses, to lead his people out of Egypt. He used a shepherd boy, David, to be king over his people. He used a prostitute, Rahab, to help capture a city from the enemy. He used an orphan daughter, Esther, to save his people from destruction. He used a baby boy, Jesus, to rescue all humanity.

God is sometimes big in small ways.

Let's turn to the stories of Gideon and David to explore this idea further.

Letters of Recommendation

Imagine if Gideon had to secure a letter of recommendation as part of an application process to be appointed the leader of God's people. I expect that it might have been something like this:

Dear God:

We're writing this letter of recommendation on behalf of Gideon. In the time that we have known him, we have found him to be fearful, timid, and withdrawn. While he's good at threshing wheat, he shows no leadership skills and is unlikely to be of any assistance to our community in the future. It is with great reservation that we would even suggest him for any future opportunities you may have in mind.

Sincerely,
The Israelites

Not the glowing recommendation that you want if you're trying to get a job or a position.

David's letter would probably not be much better.

Dear Lord:

I'm writing this letter on behalf of David, son of Jesse. I do not recommend him for position as King of Israel. He is the youngest of eight sons. He has many brothers that are clearly better suited for this all-important role. He is, after all, just a shepherd boy. And while he has been faithful to look after the family's flock, that does not mean he is ready to lead your people. Please consider one of Jesse's other sons instead.

Sincerely,
Samuel the Prophet

Again, not a real vote of confidence, is it? You'd probably want to leave that letter out of your portfolio before you applied for college or a career.

And yet, we know that God did something big in small ways through both men.

A Mighty Hero

The story of Gideon is recorded in the book of Judges. The Israelites had turned away from God and were worshipping idols and doing evil in the sight of the Lord. As a result, God handed them over to the Midianites, their enemies, for seven years. Judges 6:2-6 tell us that,

> The Midianites were so cruel that the Israelites made hiding places for themselves in the mountains, caves, and strongholds. Whenever the Israelites planted their crops, marauders from Midian, Amalek, and the people of the east would attack Israel, camping in the land and destroying crops as far away as Gaza. They left the Israelites with nothing to eat, taking all the sheep, goats, cattle, and donkeys. These enemy hordes, coming with their livestock and tents, were as thick as locusts; they arrived on droves of camels too numerous to count. And they stayed until the land was stripped bare. So Israel was reduced to starvation by the Midianites. Then the Israelites cried out to the Lord for help.

In response, the Lord sent a prophet to his people with a promise that he would deliver them from the hands of the Midianites and the Amorites, just as he had delivered them from the Egyptians.

An angel of the Lord appears to Gideon and says, "Mighty hero, the Lord is with you!"

Can you see how this scene is unfolding? Gideon is threshing wheat in a wine press. A wine press is dug down into the ground. In essence, Gideon is threshing wheat in hiding because he's fearful that the Midianites might see him and come and take his wheat. And it's in this scene that the angel of the Lord appears and announces Gideon as a "mighty hero." There is nothing in Scripture to suggest that Gideon had done anything courageous at this point.

God sees our greatness, not our weakness.

We live in a self-help and self-improvement culture that despises weakness. A weakness is a fault or a failure and therefore we must work hard to overcome our weaknesses and deficiencies in every area of our lives. The Gallup organization studied people who were successful across all industries, and they found that all successful people across all industries have one thing in common and it's not personality, leadership, intellect, charisma, or work ethic. It's this one thing: they operate in their strengths. Successful people figure out what they're good at and then they work hard at that.

That feels contrary to what I was taught in both school and church. For much of my life, it seemed my weaknesses got all the attention while my potential went untapped. And yet God does the opposite. He says of Gideon, "Mighty hero!" even though Gideon had not done anything heroic yet.

Do you see it? Can you hear God speaking to you: I know you may not have done anything yet, Mighty Hero, but I see the greatness within you.

Confidence in God

Other than John 3:16, Philippians 4:13 may be the most oft-quoted verse in the Bible. Even my favorite college football player, Tim Tebow, would write "Phil 4:13" on his eye black for nearly every game he played at the University of Florida. Paul wrote, "For I can do everything through Christ, who gives me strength." But even the sheer frequency of this verse being quoted by itself is another example of "Coffee Cup Christianity," a verse quoted out of context that misses the author's original intent. I think Philippians 4:13 has become the Christian version of "if you can dream it, you can do it." We believe we can do anything we want to do because we've got

Jesus on our side. But let's look again at what Paul is saying in the context of the verses that precede verse 13:

> Not that I was ever in need, for I have learned how to be content with whatever I have. I know how to live on almost nothing or with everything. I have learned the secret of living in every situation, whether it is with a full stomach or empty, with plenty or little. For I can do everything through Christ, who gives me strength.

Paul tells the church at Philippi that he has learned the secret of living in every situation: dependence on Christ. His confidence is in the Lord and that gives him the strength that he needs.

Joy in Hardships

> "Sir," Gideon replied, "if the Lord is with us, why has all this happened to us? And where are all the miracles our ancestors told us about? Didn't they say, 'The Lord brought us up out of Egypt'? But now the Lord has abandoned us and handed us over to the Midianites."

Notice that the angel said to Gideon, "the Lord is with *you!*" But Gideon replies, "why has all this happened to *us*?" Gideon's inclusive response illustrates that he has a heart for his people. He didn't ask, why are you doing this to *me*? Why is all this stuff happening to *me*? He says, why is this happening to *us*?

I love how the Lord responds to him. Gideon is clearly questioning God, perhaps even complaining. Where have you been? Why has all this been happening? Seriously, God, what the heck? And the Lord answers, "Go with the strength you have, and rescue Israel from the Midianites. I am sending you!"

Go with this strength you have. That fire within Gideon that challenged the Lord is a gift. The resolve he showed in hardship is good.

Our difficulties are part of the process. We're taught from the youngest age to avoid failure. Well-meaning parents often try to insulate their children from challenges and hardships, because they believe the kids can't handle disappointment and failure. Yet, the only way we learn to manage disappointment and failure is to experience disappointment and failure. The resolve and the resiliency that we develop in the process is a gift the Lord can use.

Instead, we live in a constant state of fear and anxiety, because in our Christian fantasyland, bad things don't happen to good people. We're not supposed to endure hardship or suffer. But God did not apologize to Gideon for his circumstances, instead, he instructed him to harness his passion and rescue Israel.

We grow through life's difficulties. James 1:2-4 instructs us,

Dear brothers and sisters, when troubles of any kind come your way, consider it an opportunity for great joy. For you know that when your faith is tested, your endurance has a chance to grow. So let it grow, for when your endurance is fully developed, you will be perfect and complete, needing nothing.

Wait, we're supposed to rejoice when troubles come our way?
Your girlfriend dumped you? Rejoice.
You lost your job? Rejoice.
You bombed that final exam? Rejoice.
Your best friend ghosted you? Rejoice.
This is crazy.
Why should we have great joy when we face hardships? Because we grow through life's difficulties. It's seemingly illogical, crazy even. It's such a foreign concept. We don't often understand it when

we go through trials and tribulations. In our western culture, we're great at lamentations, but lousy at celebrations. We know how to bemoan our circumstances; we don't know how to rejoice. But our joy is not to be in difficult circumstances. We rejoice because we know that God is going to do something meaningful in us because of it.

As Romans 8:28 reminds us, "God causes everything to work together for the good of those who love God and are called according to his purpose for them." Not every trial or hardship comes from the devil. Rejoice in hardships and allow God to use it for your good and the good of others.

No More Comparisons

But again, Gideon speaks from a place of insecurity.

> "But Lord," Gideon replied, "how can I rescue Israel? My clan is the weakest in the whole tribe of Manasseh, and I am the least in my entire family!" The Lord said to him, "I will be with you. And you will destroy the Midianites as if you were fighting against one man."

How many times I have responded this same way. Not me, God. Do you know who I am? Do you know my past? I'm not smart enough. I'm not good with people. I'm not as talented. I'm nobody important. Surely, you don't mean me, Lord.

But God promised Gideon, and he promises each of us, "I will be with you."

Gideon didn't think he was the right lineage or pedigree. He was from the wrong family. He was too young. But God called Samuel as a child. He called Moses in middle age. He called Abraham at the end of his life.

God doesn't have favorites.[46]

As a father, I get this. I have five children, four sons and then a daughter. If you asked me to pick my favorite, I couldn't tell you, even if you pressed me. I love them all equally, but I love them in different ways. My relationship with each one of them is different and unique and wonderful. And even though my sons would tell you that my daughter is my favorite because she gets whatever she wants, I still have no favorite.

And God feels the same way about his children. He looks across the face of the earth at his children and he says, I can't do it. I can't pick a favorite. I love them all and I love them all equally. My relationship with all of them is different and unique and wonderful. But I can't pick a favorite. I can't do it.

So, avoid comparison. In Galatians 2:6, Paul writes, "By the way, their reputation as great leaders made no difference to me, for God has no favorites." Paul recognizes that there are other church leaders admired by the people, yet he is not threatened, for he knows that God has no favorites. It doesn't matter how other students in your classes are performing, what other employees at your job are accomplishing, or what other ministry leaders in your church are doing. God delights in you as much as he delights in them. God doesn't have favorites.

A Man After God's Own Heart

In 1 Samuel 16, we read the story of David's humble beginning. God sent the prophet Samuel to the house of Jesse to anoint one of his sons to be the next king. As a father, Jesse assembles his seven oldest sons before the prophet.

---

[46] See Galatians 2:6

When they arrived, Samuel took one look at Eliab and thought, "Surely this is the Lord's anointed!" But the Lord said to Samuel, "Don't judge by his appearance or height, for I have rejected him. The Lord doesn't see things the way you see them. People judge by outward appearance, but the Lord looks at the heart." Then Jesse told his son Abinadab to step forward and walk in front of Samuel. But Samuel said, "This is not the one the Lord has chosen." Next Jesse summoned Shimea, but Samuel said, "Neither is this the one the Lord has chosen." In the same way all seven of Jesse's sons were presented to Samuel. But Samuel said to Jesse, "The Lord has not chosen any of these." Then Samuel asked, "Are these all the sons you have?" "There is still the youngest," Jesse replied. "But he's out in the fields watching the sheep and goats."

So Jesse sends for his son, David, and upon his entrance, the Lord speaks to Samuel, "This is the one; anoint him." As David stood there, Samuel anointed him with oil. And the Spirit of the Lord "came powerfully upon David from that day on."

Why did David's father not have him in the room, to begin with? How did the prophet miss it? The answer is recorded in verse seven: "People judge by outward appearance, but the Lord looks at the heart." God cares most about what's on the inside.

What would I do if God sent a prophet to my high school to anoint a leader for the next generation? Would I parade the valedictorian in front of him, citing the high GPA, the obvious intellect, and the SAT scores? It's an impressive resume. She would make an obvious choice. Or perhaps I would go get the captain of the basketball team. Strong, charismatic, with great leadership skills. He would make an excellent choice. Or maybe I should go get the talented musician that serves on the worship team and bring her because she would add great value. God could use her for sure.

And yet, if we look at the pattern throughout the Scriptures, God uses men and women of humble origins. He's not impressed by our outward doings or our perfected resumes. He's not interested in our senior superlatives and our "Most Likely to Succeed" accolades. He cares most about our hearts and where our devotion truly lies.

As I consider the resumes of Gideon and David, I don't see an account of them completing any specific preparations. We don't read of Gideon training to lead an army so he would be ready when God called. There's no record of David reading literature and studying leadership out in the field, so he'd be ready to be king when God came calling. Instead, we see only that both men were faithfully serving others. In doing so, they were ready when God called.

Faithful in Waiting

In Luke 16, we read Jesus' parable of the shrewd manager. At the end of the story, Jesus explains what we are to learn from it:

> "If you are faithful in little things, you will be faithful in large ones. But if you are dishonest in little things, you won't be honest with greater responsibilities. And if you are untrustworthy about worldly wealth, who will trust you with the true riches of heaven? And if you are not faithful with other people's things, why should you be trusted with things of your own?

Faithfulness unlocks potential. God gives us an opportunity. And when we are faithful in it, he gives us a key. We use that key to open a door and step into something new. And as we're faithful in that setting, God rewards us with another key. And it opens another door, and we step into a new adventure.

Imagine someone trapped in a room and trying to get out of it. At first, he rattles the doorknob, then fiddles with the lock. When that doesn't work, he starts banging on the door with his fists. Now he's getting frustrated. He tries to kick the door down. That doesn't work. In desperation, he starts all the way across the room and runs full-speed and shoulder-first into the door. The door was still locked. What happens to him over time? He gets tired, he gets discouraged, he gets worn down, and eventually, he just slinks to the floor and gives up. And that's how too many Christians are living their lives today. Instead of being faithful where God has us and waiting for him to give us the key, we spend all our energy trying to break down doors that God is not ready to open. And in the process, we beat ourselves up. We grow frustrated, we grow discouraged, and sadly, we often quit. Yet, if we had just waited in the right time, God would have opened the door for us.

Many today are eager to lead, but few are eager to learn. God often puts us in someone else's vineyard so that we can learn from them. Be patient in the process. Be faithful in the waiting. We want to microwave, but God wants us to marinate. To move someone from tough to tender simply takes time. We can't rush the process. Be faithful as God does his good work in you.

Through the years, people have expressed concern that I do too much—that I'm going to burn out. But I've never worried about burnout because I learned early in my adult life to stop trying to break the door down. Wait for God to give me the key. I've had seasons where I was overextended, and I've had moments of impatience too. But cooperating with God is much easier than competing with him. So, I learned to be faithful and wait.

A Life of Virtue

Does the call to faithfulness mean that developing our gifts and talents lacks merit? No, of course not. But we must remember that developing our character must take priority because God is more concerned with our character than our talent. But here's the good news. Talents are limited, but virtues are not. We are all given a measure of talents, some receive five, some two, and some only one.[47] There's only so much that we can do with our talents, but there are no limits to what we can do with our character. Every day that we get up, we can become more and more Christlike in the way that we live. Our virtue lacks no limit other than the fullness of Christ himself.

In Matthew 25, Jesus tells the parable of the three servants. He says that a man was going on a long trip and so he called his servants together and entrusted his money to them while he was to be gone. To the first, he gave five bags of silver, to the second, he gave two bags of silver, and to the third, he gave one bag of silver, dividing it in proportion to their abilities.

> The servant who received the five bags of silver began to invest the money and earned five more. The servant with two bags of silver also went to work and earned two more. But the servant who received the one bag of silver dug a hole in the ground and hid the master's money.

When the master returned, he asked the servants to give an account of what they did with his money. The servant with five bags of silver came forward with five more. The master was very pleased and exclaimed, "Well done, my good and faithful servant. You have

---

[47] See Matthew 25:14–30

been faithful in handling this small amount, so now I will give you many more responsibilities. Let's celebrate together!'

The servant with two bags of silver invested it well and brought the master two more bags of silver. The master was delighted and again exclaimed, 'Well done, my good and faithful servant. You have been faithful in handling this small amount, so now I will give you many more responsibilities. Let's celebrate together!'

Finally, the servant given one bag of silver came forward and explained, "Master, I knew you were a harsh man, harvesting crops you didn't plant and gathering crops you didn't cultivate. I was afraid I would lose your money, so I hid it in the earth. Look, here is your money back."

The master was angry with the servant and replied, "You wicked and lazy servant! If you knew I harvested crops I didn't plant and gathered crops I didn't cultivate, why didn't you deposit my money in the bank? At least I could have gotten some interest on it."

The master ordered the money to be taken from this servant and given to the one with the ten bags of silver, announcing, "To those who use well what they are given, even more will be given, and they will have an abundance. But from those who do nothing, even what little they have will be taken away."

This story, sometimes called the Parable of the Talents, isn't really about talent development but about character development. Each servant was entrusted with a differing amount of silver to invest, but the two faithful servants were given the same reward. God has entrusted us with gifts and resources that we are to steward well, and that is a matter of character, not talent. So, as you complete your college degrees and your career training opportunities, remember to be equally devoted to developing virtue along the way. Christlikeness may not get listed on your professional resume or your LinkedIn profile, but your faithfulness will be rewarded by your father in heaven.

Just Like Gideon

Is the next Gideon reading this book? Is the next David, Daniel, or Esther? Yes, yes, they are.

When I was in high school, I strived for that perfected resume. It was the only pathway I knew, and it was simple: Do well in high school so you can go to a good college. Go to a good college so you can get a good job. Get a good job so you can live in a nice house, enjoy a nice lifestyle, retire with some savings, play some golf, and die. Kind of depressing, isn't it?

I didn't understand that God had a purpose for my life and that God might want to do something in me and through me. I assumed that God called some people to be pastors. And the rest of us, we just do whatever we want and hang on until we get to heaven.

Let's not pattern our lives after the world's standard and expectations of success. Let's really commit to the ideal that our achievements, our accolades, and our aptitudes don't matter nearly as much as the attitudes of our hearts. Let us be prepared for that moment when God calls out and says to us, "Arise, for this is the one."

When I look at the story of Gideon, I see so much of myself in that story. I was just a kid from rural Summerfield, out in the country. I was shy, introverted, and nervous around people. I didn't think there was anything particularly special about me and I didn't believe that I would do anything especially important in my life. So, when my Language Arts teacher told me that I couldn't produce quality work, I believed his lie.

For the next four years of high school, I never produced a writing more than two pages in length. I did the bare minimum with the least amount of effort possible. The pattern continued for more than a decade, including undergraduate and graduate school, until God took me on a journey of redemption years later. If you would have told me in eighth grade – staring at that big red F – that one day I would write a book, I would have called you crazy. And yet, here it is in print, the restoration of a joy that was stolen from me more than thirty-five years ago. But today, I'm not even that surprised. After all, God is sometimes big in small ways.

CHAPTER SEVEN

Finish Last

There is a hashtag on social media that is used to fuel the debate about who is the #GOAT – that is, who is the Greatest Of All Time. When Tom Brady won another Super Bowl with the Tampa Bay Buccaneers, he solidified his claim at the GOAT in football. With Messi's World Cup win in 2022, many will argue that he has earned the title as the GOAT in the other football. Katie Ledecky, who won 42 medals in international competition between 2012-2022 is the GOAT in swimming and one of the greatest Olympians of all time. Every major sport has its GOAT, though the debate may never truly be settled in professional basketball, with both Michael Jordan and LeBron James considered the GOAT by fans of different eras.

We honor greatness as a virtue in western culture. We want to be the first and the best. Stories of sportsmanship give us goosebumps when we see a heartwarming gesture in a viral video on social media, but only champions get their pictures on magazine covers and cereal boxes.

When renowned boxer Cassius Clay (later Muhammed Ali) recorded these famous words in 1963, the world applauded: "I am the greatest. I said that even before I knew I was."

Hashtag GOAT.

Greatness Defined

But the GOAT debate isn't new. Nearly two thousand years ago, Jesus' disciples were having the same conversation among themselves: "Then his disciples began arguing about which of them was the greatest."[48]

If the disciples had been on Twitter, I'm sure that John the Beloved would have posted something like

#TheOneWhomJesusLoved is the #GOAT.

and Bartholomew would have tweeted

BART = #GOAT.

But Jesus catches onto the conversation and brings a little child over to his side.

Then he said to them, "Anyone who welcomes a little child like this on my behalf welcomes me, and anyone who welcomes me also welcomes my Father who sent me. Whoever is the least among you is the greatest."[49]

While traveling to Capernaum, the disciples were again arguing about which of them was the greatest, so Jesus sat them down and

---

[48] Luke 9:46

[49] Luke 9:47-48

said, "Whoever wants to be first must take last place and be the servant of everyone else."[50]

And in Matthew 18, we find the disciples asking Jesus directly, "Who is greatest in the Kingdom of Heaven?" Jesus responded by calling a little child over into their midst, and answered, "Anyone who becomes as humble as this little child is the greatest in the Kingdom of Heaven."[51]

In every instance, Jesus brought a child into the conversation. Children held the lowest status in society in the ancient world. By admonishing the disciples to "become as humble as this little child," Jesus was not pining for some innocent and idealistic faith. He was speaking of a lowly position within societal ranks. The more the disciples clamored for the top, the more Jesus insisted they seek the bottom.

According to Jesus, greatness is defined as:

1. being the least among others
2. taking last place
3. serving everyone else
4. assuming the status of a child

Who is the greatest? It's an intoxicating question, even and especially in our modern world. We couch our quest for greatness with more socially acceptable terms like success and profits and likes and subscribers. But in the end, it's still about being the #GOAT.

But remember, Jesus had something to say about goats. And it wasn't a compliment.

---

[50] Mark 9:35

[51] Matthew 18:1-2, 4

The Least of These

In Matthew 25, we read this from Jesus,

> But when the Son of Man comes in his glory, and all the angels with him, then he will sit upon his glorious throne. All the nations will be gathered in his presence, and he will separate the people as a shepherd separates the sheep from the goats. He will place the sheep at his right hand and the goats at his left.

On the day of judgment, all the nations are going to be gathered, and Jesus is going to separate them into two groups: sheep and goats. What will be the criteria he uses to divide them?

> Then the King will say to those on his right, 'Come, you who are blessed by my Father, inherit the Kingdom prepared for you from the creation of the world. For I was hungry, and you fed me. I was thirsty, and you gave me a drink. I was a stranger, and you invited me into your home. I was naked, and you gave me clothing. I was sick, and you cared for me. I was in prison, and you visited me.'

> Then these righteous ones will reply, 'Lord, when did we ever see you hungry and feed you? Or thirsty and give you something to drink? Or a stranger and show you hospitality? Or naked and give you clothing? When did we ever see you sick or in prison and visit you?'

> And the King will say, 'I tell you the truth, when you did it to one of the least of these my brothers and sisters, you were doing it to me!'

The sheep – those at his right hand – will inherit the kingdom because of their care and concern for others. But to those at his left hand – the goats – the King will say,

'Away with you, you cursed ones, into the eternal fire prepared for the devil and his demons. For I was hungry, and you didn't feed me. I was thirsty, and you didn't give me a drink. I was a stranger, and you didn't invite me into your home. I was naked, and you didn't give me clothing. I was sick and in prison, and you didn't visit me.'

Then they will reply, 'Lord, when did we ever see you hungry or thirsty or a stranger or naked or sick or in prison, and not help you?'

And he will answer, 'I tell you the truth, when you refused to help the least of these my brothers and sisters, you were refusing to help me.'

The sheep will go into eternal life, but the goats into eternal punishment. And judgment will not be based on what we believed but on how we behaved. It will be in our care for the hungry, the thirsty, the stranger, the naked, and the imprisoned. A group of people that Jesus called "the least of these."

Are we a sheep or a goat? And do we know the difference?

There was a video circulating in August 2021 of a woman who was interviewed by CNN at a political rally. When she was asked about the Covid vaccine, she told the reporter, "I think it is time where God is separating the sheep from the goats." When the reporter asked, "What are you?" she chuckled, then answered, "I'm a goat because I ain't a sheep. I'm not doing what they tell me to do."[52] I think she's forgotten to whom Jesus promises a reward.

In a *Washington Post* article from July 2018, a 67-year-old Sunday School teacher in Alabama provided clarification on some of Jesus' mandates:

Love thy neighbor, she said, meant "love thy *American* neighbor."

Welcome the stranger, she said, meant the "*legal* immigrant stranger."

"The Bible says, 'If you do this to the least of these, you do it to me,'" Sheila said, quoting Jesus. "But the least of these are *Americans*, not the ones crossing the border."[53]

This is indicative of what we can so easily do in our Christian walk. We can rationalize our personal biases and political ideologies and excuse away our actions that make us the goats that Jesus warned us about.

I don't want to live anymore as a goat. I don't want to strive to be the greatest of all time. I want to reflect the love and character of Christ to everyone, but especially to the least of these. I want to be a sheep.

I want to start a new hashtag. If Jesus defined greatness as being the least among others, then instead of being the #GOAT I want to be the #LAMB. *The Least Among Men, Baby!*

---

[52] Donie O'Sullivan, "'God is separating the sheep from the goats': Trump supporter on why she remains unvaccinated," YouTube Video, August 23, 2021, CNN, https://www.youtube.com/watch?v=Vr3ZNvv0aco.

[53] Stephanie McCrummen, "Judgment Days," Washington Post online, July 21, 2018, https://www.washingtonpost.com/news/national/wp/2018/07/21/feature/god-trump-and-the-meaning-of-morality/.

Imagine what could happen in our world if Christians embraced the notion that instead of seeking greatness (and all its euphemistic alternatives), we determined to be the least among men, to finish last, to serve others, and to humble ourselves as children.

Preloading a Response

We often know the right thing to do. The hard part is doing it. We can all remember a time when something was said or done and we failed to act, only to later experience regret. In the aftermath, we wished we would have said this or done that. But it's too late. The moment has passed.

Psychologist Peter Gollwitzer suggests having "implementation intentions" so that this doesn't happen. He recommends making advanced mental commitments. It's the idea of preloading a response.

Deciding ahead of time, that if _________ happens, I will do _________.

Studies have shown that people who use advanced mental commitments are far more likely to achieve their goals than those who do not, including a higher efficiency of students turning in homework, more loyalty to individual fitness plans, and so on.[54] We can use this strategy so that we don't encounter those regrettable moments anymore.

A few years ago, I was leaving Moe's Southwest Grill after having lunch. As I exited the parking lot, I passed a homeless man on the street with a sign that simply said "Hungry." I didn't have any money, so I kept driving. A few blocks down the road, I immediately felt a conviction that even though I didn't have any cash in my

---

[54] Chip & Dan Heath, *The Power of Moments* (New York: Simon & Schuster, 2017), 186.

wallet, I did have my debit card. I just bought one lunch. I could buy another one.

I turned around and drove back to the restaurant. Pulling up alongside the man, I rolled down my window and asked, "Hungry?"

"Yeah," he replied simply, "I haven't eaten today."

"I can buy you a lunch inside," I offered. "What do you like?"

"Steak's good," he suggested.

"Yes, yes, it is," I laughed. "Be right back."

I walked inside Moe's and ordered a big burrito with double steak, chips and salsa, and a large soda. When it was ready, I carried it outside to where he was waiting. As he ate, I sat and talked with him.

"What's your name?" I asked.

"James."

James proceeded to tell me a story of how he had made a bunch of dumb mistakes that had landed him where he was, but he was working hard to get back on his feet. He had experience in the restaurant industry, and he had job applications in at a few places, but it was hard to secure a job when there's no address to put on the application.

We talked a little longer, and then I prayed for him before I left.

As I drove away from the restaurant for the second time that day, I realized that I almost missed an opportunity to do something for the least of these. I almost drove away feeling like a sheep but acting like a goat.

I determined that I never again wanted to miss Jesus in disguise, so I preloaded this response:

If someone asks for help, then I will do whatever I have means to do.

Now, I give food or money to people who are hungry. I buy gas at the gas station for people who need it. I do whatever I can, whenever I can. Sometimes it's a lot, sometimes it's a little, and sometimes I can't do anything at all.

Two weeks after I met James, our family was headed to PDQ for lunch after church. As we waited for the green light to turn left into the parking lot, we saw a homeless man sitting on the street corner, holding up a blank piece of cardboard.

I rolled down my window and asked, "Hey, what's your sign say?"

"Nothing," he grumbled. "I don't have a pen."

"Well, you're in luck," I told him. "I got a Sharpie."

I handed him a black marker and told him he could keep it. I also told him that we were going to eat and that if he waited here for us, we would bring him back some lunch in about thirty minutes.

"Don't go anywhere," I reminded him. "We'll be back soon."

After we finished our lunches, we ordered a couple of meals to go and got a couple of bottles of water and headed back to where John was supposed to be waiting for us. But when we got there, we couldn't find him. We drove up and down the six-lane road, my kids searching for him like a real-life game of Where's Waldo. We finally found him walking along the sidewalk in front of the supermarket. We pulled into the parking lot, and I got out of the car to take John's food to him.

As we were standing there making small talk for a few minutes, I looked down and discovered that John was barefoot. The black asphalt and the concrete sidewalks get unbearably hot in the middle of a Florida summer and it is almost impossible to walk outdoors without shoes.

"John, where are your shoes?" I asked.

"I left them at a laundromat."

"What laundromat? Maybe I can get them back." But he just pointed in a nondescript direction, and I realized it was useless to pursue that idea further.

I looked at his bare feet. I looked at my shoes, making a quick comparison. Yes, these will fit, I surmised. I kicked off my shoes and offered them to John.

"Here, you can have these. You'll need them given how hot it's been this summer."

I think he was more excited about the free shoes than the free food. We talked to John about his family and his situation, and before we left, we prayed for him. We prayed that God would provide the kind of longtime help he required and send more families to meet his immediate needs in the interim. But in that moment, we did what we could do. Our preloaded response prepared us to be ready to help.

There are three objections I often hear to helping strangers in need:

1. It could be a scam. I know that there are those who don't give money to people in need because they don't know if the person is really in need. They've heard stories of people who pretend to be homeless to get money. I don't share that concern. If someone made in the image of God wants to spend every day pretending to be homeless and beg for a few dollars, I'm not the one that's being cheated in this life.

2. They might use it for drugs or alcohol. Yes, this is a possibility. If you know the person you are helping has an addiction and your money would be enabling of their dangerous habit, then don't do it. But if it's a stranger in need and there is no suspicion of substance abuse, then be generous and trust God. Once we give them the money, it's theirs to steward. If they use it to find a temporary means of relief from the pain of this life, that is their choice to make. But I committed years ago that I will do something if I have the means to do it.

3. If you don't work, you don't eat. This reference to 2 Thessalonians 3:10 is sometimes cited to suggest that we refrain from giving handouts to those in need. But Paul's criticism is of those capable of working who do not. Too often, we lean on this verse to justify not helping people in

need believing that they are lazy or freeloaders. But I have seen first-hand how difficult it can be to get a job without an address or to get an address without a job. It's a catch-22. Add in the impacts of mental illness for many in the homeless community and it's not as simple as "get a job!"

My convictions do not need to become your convictions. But what response can you preload to ensure that you don't miss an opportunity to be the #LAMB and to care for the least of these? But our responses aren't the only things that we need to preload. We must also reexamine how we approach not just success in caring for those in need, but success as a whole.

If we're not careful, our definition of success can look a lot like the vision of greatness that the disciples revered, and Jesus dismissed.

Is it time for Christians to redefine success?

Redefining Success

From age five to at least fifty, we spend the better part of our hours and days in pursuit of success. First grade school, then high school. For many, college next, then career. Along the way, we work to build homes and families and retirement accounts.

In Romans 12:2, Paul writes, "Don't copy the behavior and customs of this world, but let God transform you into a new person by changing the way you think. Then you will learn to know God's will for you, which is good and pleasing and perfect." As we used to say in children's church, "we need to change our stinkin' thinkin'" or we will unknowingly find ourselves "copying the behaviors and customs of this world."

The world defines success vertically, that is, it goes from the bottom to the top. Think about the language we use to describe success:

- climbing the corporate ladder
- moving up
- reaching new heights
- upward mobility
- at the top of his game
- working her way up
- the pinnacle of success.

This model is often embraced by well-meaning parents and educators. We want our kids to play up (if they're nine, we want them playing with eleven-year-olds.) We want our kids to test up into a higher reading group or be placed up in an advanced class. If other kids read at age five, then our kids should be reading by age four. In essence, we expect our kids to be the best athletes, dancers, or musicians; to make straight A's on their report card and 100's on their tests. We want our children to be well-mannered and not get in trouble in school so as not to cause us any embarrassment. And if they do all that, graduate with honors, go to college, earn a degree, and get a job, then we can breathe a sigh of relief and feel good about being the proud parents of a successful young man or woman. Our kids' teachers applaud us, our community commends us, and our friends congratulate us.

But what if your parents and teachers got it wrong?

I believe that the Biblical view of success is a very different model. Whereas the world defines success vertically, I believe the kingdom model of success is defined laterally. It goes from start to finish. Consider the language found in Scripture:

- "work out your salvation"[55]
- "to Him who overcomes"[56]
- "running the race"[57]
- "fight the good fight"[58]
- "narrow is the path that leads to life"[59]

These expressions suggest that the biggest achievement in life is not how high we climb, but how far we'll walk. It's not about reaching the top; it's about reaching the finish.

Jesus provides a clear picture of Kingdom success. It was not when he turned water into wine or when he taught the multitudes on the hillside or helped the disciples catch a net full of fish. It was not when he read from the scroll in the temple or when he healed the soldier's ear cut off by Peter in the garden or when he raised Lazarus from the dead.

His real crowning achievement were the thorns upon his brow and the nails in his hand. His moment of success recorded in just three simple words: "It is finished."[60] That was the pinnacle of his success. That was his climatic moment. That was what he spent his whole life preparing for. To reach the end and declare, "It is finished."

It's interesting to me that at the times when Jesus was performing all those incredible acts—healing the sick, feeding the multitudes, walking on water—his followers must have thought he was the picture of absolute success. Yet, at the crucifixion, only one was there to see him in his final moments. At the pinnacle of his

---

[55] Philippians 2:12 (NKJV)

[56] Revelation 3:21

[57] 1 Corinthians 9:24-27

[58] 1 Timothy 6:12

[59] Matthew 7:14

[60] John 19:30

greatest triumph, they all had scattered. As Jesus hung on the cross and declared his success, his disciples abandoned him, condemning him a failure.

Pursuing success begins with redefining it according to a kingdom standard. Does this mean that academic pursuits or career aspirations are unimportant? No, of course not. These things do matter. They are a part of the vocational calling we examined in Chapter Four. But I know that if we learn to pursue kingdom success and not worldly success, then all the other things that we have need of will be added unto us.[61] God will bless our hands and our labor and expand our territory.

If you never achieve success by the world's standard, it will not matter. Though others may condemn you a failure, it will not disappoint.

It's not reaching the top but reaching the finish.

It's not crying out "I have done it," but only "It is finished."

The only "attaboy" that will ever really matter: "Well done, my good and faithful servant. Let's celebrate together!"[62]

Jesus today would be seen as a CEO, sitting atop the organizational chart. And though he should be a featured executive on "Undercover Boss," it's more likely he'd be followed by Mike Rowe for an episode of "Dirty Jobs." Because Jesus wasn't afraid to get his hands dirty.

---

[61] Matthew 6:33

[62] Matthew 25:14

Washing Their Feet

John 13:3-5 states,

> Jesus knew that the Father had given him authority over everything and that he had come from God and would return to God. So he got up from the table, took off his robe, wrapped a towel around his waist, and poured water into a basin. Then he began to wash the disciples' feet, drying them with the towel he had around him.

Jesus had all authority. He's the Son of God, the King of kings, the Lord of lords. He did not have to stoop low to wash the feet of his disciples, a task that would have qualified as a "dirty job" in those days. As a kid, I used to run around barefoot everywhere, even inside convenience stores and grocery marts. (This was before the days of "no shirt, no shoes, no service.") I would come home at the end of the day and my mother would send me straight to the bathroom to wash off my "jiffy store feet," a label reserved for only the dirtiest and most disgusting feet. I imagine Jesus washing the disciples' "jiffy store feet"—covered with dirt and sweat and grime accumulated from walking outdoors with sandals day after day— and doing so with the tender care of a Savior who loved them.

As KJ Ramsey explains, "both the water of the basin and baptism soak us in the story that says you are never too dirty or undignified to be welcomed by God."[63]

When Jesus finished washing the disciples' feet, he told them, "You call me 'Teacher' and 'Lord,' and you are right, because that's what I am. And since I, your Lord and Teacher, have washed your

---

[63] KJ Ramsey, *The Lord Is My Courage*, (Grand Rapids: Zondervan, 2022), 66.

feet, you ought to wash each other's feet. I have given you an example to follow. Do as I have done to you."[64]

Jesus humbled himself in service to others—at their feet and upon the cross—and he calls us to do the same. Ramsey writes,

> He stooped down—by becoming human, by being baptized in a repentance he did not need, by giving his time and attention to those whom religious folks deemed as unworthy of belonging, by washing feet and blessing the meek. Then he climbed high, not onto a stage but to a cross, where he let his body descend to the lowest place, death itself.[65]

The #GOAT became the lamb.

---

[64] John 13:13-15

[65] Ramsey, *The Lord Is My Courage*, 65.

CHAPTER EIGHT

Keep The Beat

As a freshman in high school, I wanted to be a band director when I grew up. I started playing the piano when I was young and then learned the saxophone when I reached middle school. By my sophomore year, I was the first chair alto sax in the marching and symphonic bands and the lead tenor sax player in the school's jazz band.

In the summer between tenth and eleventh grades, our marching band traveled to Washington, DC. We had been selected to represent the state of Florida in the annual Independence Day parade in our nation's capital.

It was an incredibly memorable trip. I visited iconic sites. I toured the Smithsonian. I marched before thousands of spectators. I roomed with my best friends. I got dismissed.

Yep, at end of the trip, I was expelled from the band program. Apparently, ordering room service after curfew and listening to music instead of the tour guide were no-no's. And with that, the dream to one day be a band director died.

My favorite part about band—the reason I wanted to become a director—was the conducting. I loved holding the baton and

moving my hand in rhythm—down, in, out, up, down, in, out, up—
to keep everyone on the right beat as the music was played.

The world is full of natural rhythms too. We see this woven into
the creation account recorded in Genesis 1:

> In the beginning God created the heavens and the earth.
> The earth was formless and empty, and darkness covered
> the deep waters. And the Spirit of God was hovering over
> the surface of the waters. Then God said, "Let there be light,"
> and there was light. And God saw that the light was good.
> Then he separated the light from the darkness. God called
> the light "day" and the darkness "night."
>
> And evening passed and morning came, marking the
> first day.

Again, the next day, God spoke, and creation responded, and
God called it good.

"And evening passed and morning came, marking the second day."

This pattern was followed each day of that first week of Creation.
God established a steady rhythm—a natural cadence—and baked it
into the created order for all of eternity.

We observe it in the rhythm of the days—mornings and night,
sunrise and sunset—and the way that we navigate these days: sleep
then wake, rest then work.

We find it in the rhythm of the seasons—winter, spring, summer, fall—and the way we move within them: sowing and reaping,
planting and harvesting.

We feel it in the rhythm of our bodies—breath in, breath out—
and the steady pulse of the heartbeat inside our chest.

As humans, we translate this natural rhythmic design into the
things that we create. Rhythm is the foundation of our music. We

hum a catchy tune, but only a catchy beat makes us move our feet. The cadence of our poetry and rap turns our lonely words into lyrical notes.

When an athlete or musician or dancer finds that rare place of focus and performance—when they're in the zone—if we're present to watch, we are awed by what we see. There is something compelling and beautiful about watching others when they have found their rhythm.

As a young musician, I would often make one of four common errors that would cause me to get out of rhythm: I would either be too fast, too free, too loud, or too weak. And, if we're honest, most of us would acknowledge that we struggle to keep a steady rhythm in our personal lives. We discover that we have become too fast, too free, too loud, or too weak. We have fallen out of the natural rhythm God intended for us to enjoy. Thankfully, He has given us spiritual practices to get us back in rhythm and to help us keep the beat.

Too Fast

My first piano recital was at the end of fifth grade. My final selection was Beethoven's "Fur Elise." Once I learned to play the song, I became obsessed with playing it as quickly as I could. It was a personal challenge to test my dexterity and see how fast I could make my fingers fly across those keys without making a mistake. With some practice, I was playing it at more than three times it's intended speed. My elderly piano instructor was not impressed.

"Who wrote this music?" she asked.

"Beethoven."

"That's right," she replied. "Which means he gets to decide the tempo. And what does it say there at the top?"

"Allegro," I responded, sheepishly.

"Very good. Now, let me hear it played allegro."

With much resignation, I would slow down and play it at the tempo she wanted, though I could never understand why she didn't think playing it fast would be more impressive to the people attending the piano recital later that spring.

Life also has a way of speeding us up, and as John Mark Comer notes in his book *The Ruthless Elimination of Hurry*, there is a new epidemic of the modern world: "hurry sickness." Among the ten symptoms he associates with this disease are restlessness, workaholism, emotional numbness, escapist behaviors, and slippage of spiritual disciplines.[66] At times in my life, I would have checked off all ten boxes. I drove fast, I walked fast, I looked for the shortest checkout lines at the grocery stores. I was always in a hurry, even when I didn't have anywhere to be. I needed to learn to slow down.

On more than one occasion, I have been so busied and so hurried that I ignored the warning light in my car alerting me that my gas tank was nearing empty. I've coasted into the gas station on fumes. I've been stranded on the side of the road. And one fateful evening that my wife will never let me forget, we ran out of gas on a deserted stretch of interstate in South Florida after midnight and had to hitch a ride with a tow truck to the nearest service station.

I've learned my lesson. Now, when I get below a quarter of a tank, I find a gas station and fuel up.

In the same way, the practice of Sabbath helps us to slow down so we can fill up. It's a weekly discipline that acts as a reset button on our hurried lives. It's a time to fuel up so we're not running on empty.

Sabbath comes from the Hebrew word *shabbat*, which means to stop. We stop working, we stop studying, we stop striving, and we stop wanting. We cease from our doing so that we can slow down and fill up.

---

[66] John Mark Comer, *The Ruthless Elimination of Hurry* (Colorado Springs: Waterbook, 2019), 46-51.

The Fourth Commandment instructs us in the practice of Sabbath:

> Remember to observe the Sabbath day by keeping it holy. You have six days each week for your ordinary work, but the seventh day is a Sabbath day of rest dedicated to the Lord your God. On that day no one in your household may do any work. This includes you, your sons and daughters, your male and female servants, your livestock, and any foreigners living among you. For in six days the Lord made the heavens, the earth, the sea, and everything in them; but on the seventh day he rested. That is why the Lord blessed the Sabbath day and set it apart as holy.[67]

We get six days to do our ordinary work, but the Lord said that the seventh day is different. It is "a day of rest dedicated to the Lord." Sabbath is more than just a day off. It is a 24-hour period of rest and worship. Does that mean that we should spend the whole time sleeping or singing Chris Tomlin songs? No, rest takes many forms besides a nap, and worship takes many forms besides singing. We'll explore that more later in this chapter.

Pastor and spiritual formation expert Rich Villodas writes, "You could argue that the commandment most violated by everyone is the fourth. It's also the commandment we often boast about breaking in our pride to express how tirelessly we work. Yet our lives are under the judgment of our own frenetic pace because we can't stop."[68]

I know that there may be some who would say, "Wait, but Sabbath—that's in the Old Testament. We don't follow the Old Testament anymore. Jesus came and we live in the era of the New

---

[67] Exodus 20:8-11

[68] Rich Villodas, *The Deeply Formed Life* (Colorado Springs: Waterbrook, 2020), 30.

Testament." In truth, I held that view for most of my life. Sabbath was two hours of church, not twenty-four hours of rest.

But Sabbath pre-dates the Ten Commandments. In fact, it even pre-dates the Fall. God worked for the first six days of creation and rested on the seventh day. If God rested from his work, how much more should we? John Mark Comer argues, "When we fight this work-six-days, Sabbath-one-day rhythm, we go against the grain of the universe."[69]

Sabbath is not a reward for checking off everything on the to-do list. We'll rest, but only after we finish that presentation, clean the apartment, submit that assignment, answer those emails, visit the gym, make that Target run, and pay those bills. Instead, we must rest from our work so that we can work from a place of rest.

I used to rest only after I got all my work done. So, I never rested. There was always more to do. But a Stanford study led by Professor John Pencavel found a sharp decline in productivity when a person worked over 50 hours a week. Beyond the 55 hour-mark, productivity decreased so much that any extra hours worked became pointless.[70] Fifty hours is the equivalent of about six eight-hour workdays. Working on the seventh day, instead of resting, is less productive.

Jesus said that "The Sabbath was made to meet the needs of people, and not people to meet the requirements of the Sabbath."[71] I don't keep the Sabbath because it's a rule, but because it's a gift. It was "made to meet the needs of people," and I desperately need it.

To get started with a Sabbath rhythm, try this:

---

[69] Comer, *The Ruthless Elimination of Hurry*, 153.

[70] Neeramitra Reddy, "A Stanford Study Reveals the Perfect Number of Hours You Should Work Every Week," Medium, April 8, 2022, https://medium.com/wholistique/a-stanford-study-reveals-the-perfect-number-of-hours-you-should-work-every-week-1dd98044d11f.

[71] Mark 2:27

1. Choose a day. Traditionally, the Sabbath was observed from Friday night to Saturday night, but I don't think the day matters as much as what you commit to do on that day. Our family practices Sabbath from 6:00 p.m. Saturday night, to 6:00 p.m. Sunday night. We chose this day because we wanted church to be a part of our Sabbath ritual and we attend service on Sunday mornings.

2. Plan for it. When we first added Sabbath to our weekly schedule, it was challenging. We had to plan and prepare. I couldn't spend a lazy Saturday sleeping late and then lounging on the couch watching college football all day if I wanted to be able to rest on Sunday. Instead, we needed to do our grocery shopping, clean the house, finish the laundry, and do all the other necessary chores. Sometimes it means saying no to social events on Saturdays so that we can be ready for Sabbath by evening. But with everything done, we'd sit down to dinner together at 6:00 p.m., light a Sabbath candle, and give thanks to God for an opportunity to slow down.

3. Make time for rest and worship. What kinds of things can you do during your Sabbath? Here's a list of some of what our family enjoys:
   - Go for a walk.
   - Read the Bible.
   - Have face-to-face conversations.
   - Play games.
   - Read a book.
   - Bake cookies.
   - Go to church.
   - Explore nature.
   - Pray.
   - Take a nap.
   - Do a puzzle.
   - Make art.

- Watch the birds.
- Play Pickleball.

Here's the thing: it's not law. If it's life-giving, then do it. If it's life-draining, then don't do it. If it helps you to feel refreshed, go for it. It if leaves you weary, don't do it. If it draws you closer to God, yes. If it pulls you away from Him, probably no.

For example, one of the things that I try to do is to turn off my phone and put it away for Sabbath. As much as I like being connected to the world, by Sunday, my phone is not life-giving: it's life-draining. Remember, Sabbath is a gift from God to help us to slow down and fill up. That often means turning off our devices.

When we are saying goodbye, we might wish another, "Good night!" or "Have a nice evening." In Jewish tradition, they will wish each other well on the Sabbath by saying, "*Shabbat, Shalom.*"

May you flourish from your rest and worship. May your Sabbath bring you shalom. Amen.

Too Free

Shortly after graduating from college, I decided I wanted to learn to play the guitar. I was attending a church that used contemporary worship songs, and I thought it would be cool to be able to play and sing those songs alone in my apartment and not just in Sunday services. I picked up a guitar at a local pawn shop, bought a chord book, and hit up a friend for a few lessons to get started.

Within a few weeks, I had figured out the basics and was able to play most of the chords needed for the worship songs I was trying to learn. What I struggled with were the strum patterns. I could never quite get a consistent pattern going and would sometimes even skip a few beats because I was strumming the wrong way and getting off beat. At first, I didn't notice. When it was just me at home playing and singing, I just rolled with it as I went along. But I remember the first time I got together with my friend and we tried to play together. He had the correct strum pattern for the songs, but I did not. I was way too free with my strumming and that became clear when we both played the same song at the same time. We were definitely not in unison. It wasn't enough that I knew the right chords to play, I didn't know the proper way to strum the guitar. As a result, I couldn't join in with others. It was only me and my guitar, and that was a lonely place to be.

If we are going to claim the name of Christ, we must abandon our desire for freedom for the sake of unity and community. Too many "Christians" today are living too free, saying and doing whatever they will with little regard for God's purpose and design.

This is why we need the Scriptures. It provides the metanarrative—the Big Story—that helps us to stay grounded in the faith. Paul wrote to Timothy,

> All Scripture is inspired by God and is useful to teach us what is true and to make us realize what is wrong in our lives. It corrects us when we are wrong and teaches us to do what is right. God uses it to prepare and equip his people to do every good work.[72]

Remember, as we discussed in Chapter Two, following Jesus is not about learning to live rightly, but to love rightly. The Scriptures, therefore, are not simply a moral code to be followed, but a guide to help us rightly reflect God's love and character into the world.

Theologian N.T. Wright offers a helpful metaphor. He suggests that we can view the Scriptures like a five-act play, with the first four acts being Creation (I), Fall (II), Israel (III), and Jesus (IV).

---

[72] I Timothy 3:16-17

The early church of the New Testament would be the first scenes of Act V. Wright explains,

> It would consist in the fact of an as yet unfinished drama, which contained its own impetus, its own forward movement, which demanded to be concluded in the proper manner but which required of the actors a responsible entering in to the story as it stood, in order first to understand how the threads could appropriately be drawn together, and then to put that understanding into effect by speaking and acting with both innovation and consistency.[73]

As players in the Grand Story, it should be our intent to learn the script's origin and plot and then to improvise accordingly in moving the story toward its finale.

A few years ago, I took some of my colleagues to the SAK Comedy Lab in Orlando. SAK is a leader in improv comedy and this night did not disappoint. Like the popular TV show "Whose Line Is It Anyways?" SAK actors make up the whole show on the spot with some direction and topics provided by the live audience.

On this night, I had a special surprise planned. My buddy Justin coaches high school boys basketball and his team had won a state championship a few weeks prior. To celebrate, I signed up Justin for an Improv Special at SAK. Midway through the performance, they announced Justin as a special guest and invited him on to the stage. A few weeks before our visit, I had filled out a basic questionnaire about Justin and his coaching endeavors, and the actors reviewed that with him on stage. They asked a few additional questions, including some details about some of the players on his team. Then, they sent Justin back to his seat as they introduced the audience to "Coach Harden: The Musical."

---

[73] N.T. Wright, "How Can the Bible be Authoritative?" Vox Evangelica 21 (1991): 7-32.

For the next ten minutes, we watched a group of actors who knew very little about Justin (or evidently about basketball in general) perform a hilarious original story about Justin and his championship team. It was funny because it was believable. There was enough truth in it, even if exaggerated for comedic effect, that we couldn't help but laugh and point and nod.

Without reading the detailed answers on the questionnaire that I completed and without spending time getting to know Justin a little bit, the actors could not have played it well. If they had just decided to do a musical about basketball as a general topic, it may have still been funny, but it would not have represented Justin, and the audience would have never heard about the great exploits of Coach Harden. While the actors took some liberties, if they had been too free, it would have failed.

You can't play the part if you don't read the script.

Jeremy Myers writes, "In this way, the Bible guides and informs us, not so that we mindlessly repeat what other characters in the story have said and done, but so that we allow the previous Acts in the story to inform and guide what we ourselves say and do in our part of the story.

Some of the things will be similar, but most will be different, and everything will build upon what has come before to carry the plot forward toward the appropriate conclusion."[74]

When Christians don't read the script, one of two things happens:

1. They get stage fright. When they are asked to play their part—to embody their faith in the public eye—they freeze. When they are finally given an opportunity to deliver their lines, they stand silently, too afraid to speak. Their witness is lost in the moment.

---

[74] Jeremy Myers, "How to Properly Read the Story of Scripture," Redeeming God online, https://redeeminggod.com/how-to-properly-read-the-story-of-scripture/.

2. They monologue. They don't know what to say so they just babble on endlessly trying to fill the air while they search for the right words, but never find them. TV personalities on air, politicians at debates, and experts-who-aren't-really-experts giving interviews, will often resort to monologuing because they never bothered to learn their lines. In the same way, we can fall "out of character" if we aren't intentional about staying true to the script.

Have you ever watched someone fumbling through a live event on stage, whether a performance or public speaking? Maybe a stand-up comic who's bombing or a senior pastor who's ill-prepared? The experience is just as uncomfortable for the audience members as it is for the person on stage. When Christians get stage fright or resort to monologuing, the world endures it awkwardly too. Instead of an artful appreciation for the Christian witness, it's met with a nervous uncertainty or mocking criticism.

The Playwright has cast us each into a role. Let us not be too free that we would fail to find our voice and play our part in the greatest story ever told.

Too Loud

Early in my teaching career, I attended a lot of our high school basketball games, so I thought it would be fun to form a Pep Band to play at home games. I reached out to some other teachers and friends, and we quickly put together a small ensemble –trumpets, saxophones, flutes, and a drum kit. I played the trumpet, but not well. I only knew one volume. LOUD. The only way I could play the right notes was to play loudly, so I did. Which is fine when you have the melody but it's a problem when the flutes have the melodic line, and the trumpet is only playing whole notes underneath. I blasted those notes and drowned out the melody.

Life has a way of making us live loudly, yet God speaks in a gentle whisper.[75] Prayer helps us to quiet ourselves so that we can commune with the Lord. Entire books have been written about prayer and my intent here is not to provide an exhaustive study of the subject, but instead to share one truth that changed the way that I have prayed. I learned it from the model prayer that Jesus provided,

> Our Father in heaven,
> Hallowed be Your name.
> Your kingdom come.
> Your will be done
> On earth as it is in heaven.
> Give us this day our daily bread.
> And forgive us our debts,
> As we forgive our debtors.
> And do not lead us into temptation,
> But deliver us from the evil one.
> For Yours is the kingdom and the power and the glory forever. Amen.[76]

Jesus said that when we address God in prayer, we should begin, "Our Father." While we've become accustomed to this language in our modern Western culture, it would have been shocking to the disciples when they heard it.

---

[75] I Kings 19:12

[76] Matthew 6:9-13 (NKJV)

As Tyler Stanton writes,

The big question in ancient days wasn't, "Does God exist?" It would be foolish to ask such a question. "Of course God exists! Open your eyes, man! He's the cylindrical pillar of fire stretching from the desert floor into the night sky and serves as our trail guide!" Instead, the existential question in ancient days was, "Is God *knowable*?" Because a pillar of fire doesn't provoke doubt, but neither does it provide intimacy.[77]

When we pray, we talk with a Daddy, not a deity. We talk with a God who is knowable. I used to begin a prayer by addressing God as "Lord" or "Almighty God," but now I start, "Father in heaven," to remind myself of this simple truth.

I have five children. My youngest, Darcy, is my only daughter. Like most dads with their daughters, I am totally smitten with her, and I pretty much give her whatever she wants. She has me wrapped around her little finger, and I won't even deny it. I absolutely delight in her! I have nicknames for her, like Doodle and Pumpkin, and I love listening to her tiny voice when she tells me stories. We snuggle every night before bed, and she shares with me everything that she did during her day. She is not perfect, but she is my beloved daughter, and there is nothing she could do to make me love her more, and there is nothing she could do to make me love her less.

When I prayed, "Almighty God," I believed that I was addressing a disappointed God, one angry at me for my sinfulness, my unfaithfulness, and my lack of spirited devotion. But praying, "Father in heaven," I am reminded that He is a God who delights in me, even in my worst moments.

---

[77] Tyler Staton, *Praying Like Fools, Living Like Monks* (Grand Rapids: Zondervan, 2022), 56.

As children, if we did something wrong and we thought our parents were going to be angry and disappointed, we often tried to hide our wrongdoing. But if we believed our parents delighted in us, and understood our capacity to make mistakes, then we would be more likely to go and tell them the truth.

Recently, my daughter was playing Monopoly in her bedroom with her cousins, and something happened. The game board broke, and she was worried. I even overheard her say, "I think he's going to kill us." Yet, she brought the broken board to me on our living room couch, and confessed, "We folded it the wrong way, and the cardboard broke in half, and now it's in two pieces."

"That's okay, Pumpkin, it's just a game," I assured her. "We can fix it."

Rather than hiding what was broken, my daughter brought it to me. Even though she felt shame, she knew in her heart she was safe.

We all face this sin/shame dilemma, and we must decide which way we will run.

We run from the one who is disappointed; we run to the one who is delighted.

In your brokenness, don't run from God. Run to Him, the Father who delights in you.

But even when we hide, our Father comes looking for us. When Adam and Eve ate the fruit of the forbidden tree, they experienced shame for the first time, and they hid from God. So, He went looking for them, calling out for them until He found them.

We know from John 3:16 that because of God's love for the world that He willingly gave His Son, but I think the verse that follows is equally important: "For God did not send His Son into the world to condemn the world, but that the world through Him might be saved."[78]

---

[78] John 3:17 (NKJV)

When we experience sin and shame, we don't have to run and hide from God. We can run to Him because he is a Father who delights in us as his children. But even when we don't run to Him, He sent Jesus after us, not to condemn, but to save.

My friend Moe was a competitive cyclist as a teen. He was a sincere Christian growing up, but he struggled with pornography after being introduced to it via porn magazines at age nine. But at fourteen, Moe had been porn-sober for several years, and at the same time, had become quite successful on the national cycling circuit. In Moe's young mind, his success was linked to God's favor on him for not looking at pornography anymore. But on the eve of Nationals, he was out for a training ride when he spotted a magazine on the side of the road. He knew what it was. He stopped, picked it up, and took it back to his room. No longer porn-sober, Moe woke up the next morning convinced God had now removed His favor from him and he would no longer have that competitive edge that had propelled him to earlier wins. With shame weighing heavily upon him, Moe pedaled out of the starting gate in the national time trials. After a few minutes, Moe looked back to see that the next rider had already closed the gap between them. Moe was going to lose.

Until Jesus showed up.

Moe describes a vision in that moment in which he sees Jesus ride by him on a bicycle. He positioned himself just ahead of Moe and called over his shoulder, "Get on my wheel." Moe focused on that rear wheel and pedaled as hard as he could to keep pace with Jesus for the rest of the race. When he reached the finish line and the results were announced, Moe had won the national championship.

God doesn't wink at our sin. But he doesn't abandon us because he's disappointed either. He sent Jesus to lead us. Get on his wheel.

Jesus said, "Pray like this: Our Father in heaven."

Following this example, before we get into God's power or His holiness, before we petition Him with our needs, or seek His deliverance from evil, we are to first address Him as Father.

The Didache was a guide used by the early Church that predates the Bible. It called for the people to pray the Lord's prayer three times each day: morning, noon, and night. If you need to jumpstart your prayer life, consider this first step. Pray the Lord's Prayer and then begin to expand upon each line. Speak to God out of your heart, talking to a Daddy, not just a deity.

Too Weak

When our high school band marched onto the field at halftime of the Friday night football games, the percussion section would drum to keep everyone on beat. The bass drum was the center piece. These drummers had to pound out the cadence so that the hundred-plus members of the band could hear it and march in rhythm. We had a freshman on bass drum one year and he played timidly. Rather than beating the drum with authority, he struck it weakly. The rest of us couldn't hear the bass drum and found it difficult to keep the beat. We ended up out of step with one another.

In our Life is Good™ moments, it's easy to get too fast, too loud, and too free. But we also have those days and weeks and more when life isn't good, and our spiritual vibrancy gets too weak.

When life beats us down, worship lifts us up.

No one understood this better than David.

In I Samuel 21, we find David on the run. Saul is trying to kill him. David begs for bread from Ahimelech the priest. He pretends to be insane, "scratching on doors and drooling down his beard"[79] to evade King Achish of Gath, and finally escapes to the cave of Adullam. But he wasn't alone there for long, for "others began coming—men who were in trouble or in debt or who were just discontented—until David was the captain of about 400 men."

---

[79] I Samuel 21:13

David is the future king. He has been anointed by the prophet Samuel. He has defeated Goliath. And yet, here he was hiding out in a cave, and not a palace, likely frustrated with his circumstances at that moment. But he's not alone. He's keeping company with others who are discontented too.

The cave of Adullam has become the cave of Discontent.

As the adage goes, misery loves company. I can only imagine the conversations around the campfire with David and those 400 men in the cave, one-upping each other with tales of woes, and bemoaning everything wrong in their worlds. We don't know what was said or how long David dwelt in that cave, but regarding this season of his life, he wrote:

I will praise the Lord at all times.
 I will constantly speak his praises.
I will boast only in the Lord;
 let all who are helpless take heart.
Come, let us tell of the Lord's greatness;
 let us exalt his name together.
I prayed to the Lord, and he answered me.
He freed me from all my fears.
Those who look to him for help will be radiant with joy;
 no shadow of shame will darken their faces.
In my desperation I prayed, and the Lord listened;
 he saved me from all my troubles.
For the angel of the Lord is a guard;
 he surrounds and defends all who fear him.
Taste and see that the Lord is good.
Oh, the joys of those who take refuge in him!

> Fear the Lord, you his godly people,
> for those who fear him will have all they need.
> Even strong young lions sometimes go hungry,
> but those who trust in the Lord will lack no good thing.[80]

With the world beating him down, David worshipped God. David described himself here as one who was helpless, fearful, and desperate, and yet declared, "taste and see that the Lord is good" because "those who trust in the Lord will lack no good thing."

Worship is not reminding God how great He is, it's reminding us how great God is. When we worship—whether in song or reading or prayer—we are declaring who He is. In doing so, we remember who we are and whose we are. "Come, let us tell of the Lord's greatness; let us exalt his name together," David sang.

One summer, my wife and I went on a Caribbean cruise. We were scheduled to visit Grand Cayman as one of the ports of call, and being a certified diver, I knew I wanted to book a scuba excursion to see Cheeseburger Reef during our stop. When we disembarked at Georgetown, we took the short walk to the dive center near the port. Cheeseburger Reef is right off the coast, so there's no need for a boat to reach the dive spot. You can swim to it direct from the shore.

As I was getting suited up with the other divers, I noticed storm clouds starting to roll in from the horizon. The wind was picking up and we could hear thunder in the distance. As we waded into the water from the boat ramp, the waves were picking up, tossing us around while we tried to get our masks and fins on. Then the rain started. Yet, our dive instructor urged us on, so we swam atop the rough waters for about fifty yards. But as we swam, my disappointment and anger were growing. This is not what it was supposed to be like. This is the Caribbean! I was expecting warm sunshine and

---

[80] Psalm 34:1-10

balmy breezes and colorful coral reefs. Instead, I get rain clouds and wind gusts and lightning strikes overhead.

I was floating in a sea of discontent.

The instructor gave the signal for descent. I released the air from my flotation device and began to sink below the surface. It was amazing. This was the Caribbean that I was promised. This was the colorful coral reef and aquatic life that I had hoped for. There, thirty feet below the surface, the world looked so different. The anxiety above replaced by a tranquility below. Everything had changed, and yet, nothing had changed. When I turned to look back at the surface, I could still see the rain pelting the water and the lightning flashing overhead. The storms were still present up above, but now I had a new perspective. For the next 45 minutes, I explored Cheeseburger Reef with a heart full of gratitude and awe.

Worship allows us to descend into the goodness of God. To find peace in the storm. Worship doesn't change our circumstances, but it can change our perspective. David turned the cave of Discontent into a cave of Praise with this reminder: "The Lord is close to the brokenhearted; he rescues those whose spirits are crushed."[81] When life beats us down, worship lifts us up.

Taste, and see that the Lord is good.

The Conductor

My high school band director would stand on a large platform at the front of our rehearsal space waving his hands in rhythm to keep us playing together. But every so often, he would bang his baton on his music stand, and shout, "stop, stop, stop!" until the room had quieted.

---

[81] Psalm 34:18

"I thought that we were all Americans," he would exclaim, "but someone in the trumpet section is Russian." (This was his dad joke way of chiding us for playing too fast, i.e., "rushing.")

My band director helped me discover my passion for music. He taught me to play the instruments that I loved most. Like all good conductors, he followed the composer's directions in leading a body of differing people and instruments and sounds to create something artful and beautiful. He cultivated unity and helped us to keep the beat.

I liked rehearsing solo pieces on my saxophone for competition, but nothing beat playing in the band. Whether marching with my alto sax on the football field or serenading with my tenor sax in the jazz ensemble, the band community was at the heart of it all. A musician without a band is like a child without a family.

We will never be fully formed outside of community. Therefore, it is my habit to go to church every Sunday.

I know the criticisms of the Church. I've listened to the stories of friends. I've read the books and downloaded the podcasts. Yes, there has been abuse and corruption and greed and moral failure and hypocrisy. But don't quit church, find a new one. Don't give up on shepherds, find a better one.

If I eat at a restaurant and I don't like the food or I don't like the service, I don't quit on food. I find somewhere else to eat next time.

Being a part of the Church is about belonging. The early Church saw salvation as a communal experience. Baptism was an initiation into a community. We are saved from our sins, but we are saved into a community.

There are those who will go to church to get something. They go "ready to receive" or to "get fed." This sometimes leads us to say, "I didn't really get anything out of church today," but that reflects the consumerist mentality that plagues the American church. The early Church didn't gather to get anything.

There are those who will go to give. They pursue opportunities to serve, to pour out, to be a blessing.

I often get something when I go to church. I often give something when I go to church.

But I go neither to get nor to give. I go to belong.

Join a people who are working together to make something artful and beautiful. Find a conductor who will encourage you in living a life in rhythm. Find a church community where you can belong.

Sabbath creates the margin.
Scripture reveals the mystery.
Worship provides the ministry.
Prayer unveils the mystical.
Church produces the motivation.

And on one dreadful day, I needed them all.

A Terrible, Horrible, No Good, Very Bad Day

In the middle of writing this book, I was also struggling with some trauma-induced anxieties. One night, I received a series of text messages that triggered all sorts of anxious feelings. The texts were innocuous for the most part, but that didn't matter. The sender and the context were enough that my mind and body started shutting down. When I woke up the next morning, I felt paralyzed. As I drove to work, I just kept thinking, "I am broken. This person has broken me."

When I pulled into my parking space at school, I didn't get out. I sat in my car for thirty minutes, trying to process how I was feeling and make sense of why I felt so anxious. After a half an hour, it was evident that I wasn't going to be able to function at work, so I texted my team that I was taking a personal day, and I drove off.

I ended up at a prayer trail on a local church campus. I grabbed my phone, my Airpods, and my Bible, and started walking the wooded path. At first, I just listened to worship music. I couldn't even bring myself to sing or pray. I needed to be reminded again about the goodness of God. I just listened and allowed the words to soothe my soul.

After some time, I began to sing too. Then, I turned to the Scriptures and found encouragement in Psalms 23 and 34 as I read them over and over. After nearly two hours of walking and listening and singing and reading, I began to pray to my father in heaven and express everything that I was feeling in that moment.

In prayer, I felt like God directed me to call a local counselor. He agreed to see me later that day. In my session with him, I was able to work through the anxiety I was feeling and to name it. In naming it, I was able to give it to Jesus.

When the day began, I was a complete mess. By day's end, I was back in rhythm.

What helped me were the spiritual disciplines.

I found time and space to seek the Lord in a Sabbath.

I gained a renewed faith and a better perspective through worship.

I was reminded of my place in God's story and His great love for me in Scripture.

I connected with a Daddy who delights in me and hears my cries through prayer.

I found a place of belonging and a shepherd to care for me in the Church.

At our school, we sometimes divide expectations into two groups—must-do's and may-do's—to guide students in what they should be working on and in what order.

For too long, the spiritual disciplines have been presented by church leaders as must-do's, and failure to do them consistently has been met with shame and derision.

The only must-do's for the Christian are to love the Lord with all of our hearts and to love our neighbor as ourselves. In doing so, we fulfill all the law and the prophets.

The spiritual disciplines are may-do's that equip us for the must-do's.

Worship and prayer are not a got-to, they're a get-to. Sabbath and Scripture and Church are not an obligation; they are a gift.

May these gifts bring you grace and peace as you seek to find your rhythm and keep the beat.

CHAPTER NINE

Hold The Rope

For years, I had read the tragic newspaper stories about local scuba divers who got lost in a cave and drowned. I just never thought I would be one of them.

My senior year in high school, I went scuba diving at a beautiful local spring near my hometown in North Central Florida. At age 15, I had gotten certified and I would frequently dive the area springs around my home. On this particular day, I was with my best friend and the divemaster I had studied under during certification. We were going to dive Blue Grotto Springs in Williston, Florida.

Blue Grotto is an interesting diving experience. It's a large, clear spring with a water temperature of 72 degrees. It's a popular diving destination for scuba classes to use in performing their checkout dives for certification.

We arrived at Blue Grotto on a cool mid-morning, got checked in at the office, and suited up in our gear. I seldom wear a wetsuit when diving in the springs, but on this cool February morning, I was eager for a little extra help staying warm. We connected our regulators to our air tanks, strapped our vests onto the tanks, put the gear on our backs and carried our masks, snorkel, and fins as we walked down the twenty or so steps to the water's surface.

The three of us entered the water, taking a moment to adjust as the cold water filled our wetsuits. (Wetsuits are great, but it takes time for your body to heat the water trapped inside the suit. Until then, it's cold!) We inflated our vests to float at the surface, while we made final preparations. To keep my mask from fogging up, I spit on the inside of the glass and wiped it around with my finger before rinsing it out, then slipped it over my face and put on my fins.

After we had each given the "OK" signal, we released the air from our vests and began the descent to a training platform at a depth of 20 feet. From there, we could look and see a large cavern opening, spanning more than 50 feet in width. We swam into the cavern and descended to a depth of 50 feet to a large rock formation called Peace Rock (because it has a large peace sign carved into it.) Even from this depth, we could look back to the surface and the water was so clear and the visibility was so perfect that we could still see the leaves on the trees hanging over the water's edge.

This is when the dive got really interesting. From Peace Rock, we entered a small cave opening single file; Divemaster in the front, me second, and my best friend in the rear. The cave's path leads down to a depth of about 100 feet, then winds back up and out on the other side in the shape of a U. As we entered the cave, all of the natural light from the surface began to disappear as we descended alone in the darkness. Divemaster clicked on his high-powered flashlight and for a moment, we could see again. Swimming in that cave was like driving down a dark road on a starless night with only your car's headlamp leading the way. Divemaster was the only one with a flashlight, so we stayed close.

We followed the lights, sinking slowly into the depths and into the dark. 50 feet. 60 feet. 70 feet. All I could hear was the sound of my breathing through the regulator – a deep inhale – then the sound of bubbles rushing out as I exhaled. Think Darth Vader breathing, but underwater.

We continued downward. 80 feet. 90 feet. 100 feet. And finally, we arrived at the bottom. I reached behind me and checked my gauge. We were just over 100 feet below the surface. It was both an exhilarating and frightening experience to be there. I'd never been that deep before and I'd never been inside a cave. (And the truth is, I wasn't supposed to be because I was not certified for this depth or for caves!)

Because of the depth of the dive and the effects of the immense pressure on our bodies, we could only stay down there for a few minutes without risking injury when we resurfaced. So we agreed to only spend a few minutes checking out the fossil formations on the cave walls illuminated by the flashlight. I was fascinated by one such formation and I gently ran my fingers over it to feel its texture.

And then, suddenly, everything went dark. I couldn't see my best friend behind me. I couldn't see my Divemaster in front of me. I couldn't see the glow of the high-powered flashlight. I couldn't see my hand in front of my mask.

I was now utterly disoriented inside a cave that I didn't know, more than 100 feet underwater, surrounded by blackness and completely on my own. I knew from my training that I could only remain at this depth for a short period of time and that I had a limited air supply which I was then using at an increasingly faster rate.

There was only one thought running through my mind as I sat suspended in the dark and foreign waters at that moment – "What am I going to do?"

A New World

I was in my late twenties—recently married and starting a new career—when 9/11 happened, an event that fundamentally changed the world in which we live. And then, 18 years later—leading a school and a family of seven—when a global pandemic erupts and fundamentally changes again the world in which we live.

We all endure these life-altering moments, sometimes big, sometimes small. A parent's death. A cancer diagnosis. A broken engagement. A new major. A new city. A new job. We're moving joyfully through life, full of hopes and dreams for tomorrow.

And then, suddenly, everything goes dark. And we're left asking, "What am I going to do?"

Finding God on my Spotify

At The Rock School, where I serve as Headmaster, I preach a sermon series in our K-12 Chapel service each year entitled, "Finding God on my Spotify."[82] It's usually one of the most popular sermon series I do. And I think that's because music is inherently powerful.

We often associate moments in our life with a particular song.

For me, Madonna's "Crazy for You" will always remind me of my first middle school crush.

Kenny Roger's "The Gambler" brings to mind Saturday fishing trips with my Grandpa as a kid.

Michael Jackson's "Thriller" makes me wince as I think back on that fifth-grade talent show.

And I relive my first dance with my wife on our wedding day every time I hear "The Way You Look Tonight."

At my high school, one of the senior traditions was that each class would vote on a Senior Song. It was usually something popular at the time that captured the spirit of the graduating class.

---

[82] 1 Hat tip to Pastor Brian Zahnd at Word of Life Church in St. Joseph, MO, for this. His sermon series each August entitled "Find God on My iPod" was the inspiration for my Chapel series.

For my senior class, it was Nirvana's "Smells Like Teen Spirit." I can still hear my classmates shouting out the chorus along with Kurt Cobain's invocation to entertain us.

I'm not really sure what it says about my senior class that we picked that song. (I'm also not sure what it says about me that I still remember the lyrics!)

But might I suggest to you, reader, that if you were to mark this season of your life with a song, that you might consider "The Blessing" by Bethel Worship.

"The Blessing" is simply the words from the book of Numbers, Chapter 6, set to music.

Scripture says that the Lord spoke to Moses and told him to tell Aaron to say to the people:

"May the Lord bless you and keep you,

May he make his face to shine upon you and be gracious to you,

May he lift up his countenance upon you and give you peace."[832]

At this moment in history when this blessing was bestowed, the Israelites had been delivered from Egypt, crossed the Red Sea, and had been camped at Mount Sinai for about a year. But God instructed them that it was time to go. To continue through the wilderness on the way to the promised land.

The first ten chapters of the book of Numbers details the preparation for the journey. How the people were to consecrate themselves and the tabernacle and get ready. But right in the midst of this, the Lord speaks a blessing to the people. It is a blessing for a journey.

The people are leaving Mt. Sinai, the place of divine revelation. It is the place where the people received the law and the ten commandments. They are entering into the wilderness. The wilderness is the place of testing. Even Jesus entered the wilderness to be tested before beginning his journey.

---

[832] Numbers 6:24-26 (NKJV)

The people are about to leave the place of comfort, safety, and refuge. The place of divine connection with God and enter into the unknown. They were likely anxious and worried. And probably asking themselves, "What am I going to do?"

So the Lord speaks a blessing for the journey. He says six things He will do. Six reminders that God will still be present with His people on their journey.

And they are six reminders that God will still be present with you on your journey.

1. May the Lord bless you – a reminder that God is at work in you.
2. May the Lord keep you – a reminder that God protects you.
3. May He make His face shine upon you – a reminder that God smiles on you. He is glowing, not glaring!
4. May He be gracious to you – a reminder that God takes care of you.
5. May He lift up His countenance upon you – a reminder that God always has His eye on you.
6. May He give you peace – a reminder that God desires for you to flourish; to be at peace with God, creation, neighbor, and self.

Many are leaving the comfort and safety of school or home or familiarity. You are departing your Mt. Sinai to enter the wilderness because that is the only way to reach the promised land that God has for you.

What am I going to do?

Hold the Rope

As I floated in the darkness of that cave in a hundred feet of water wondering what to do, I remembered seeing a guide rope attached to the wall of the cave. So I desperately began swimming and grasping in the dark, trying to find that rope. Swimming and grasping, swimming and grasping. Until finally, my hand found the rope. Then, hand over hand, I followed that rope forward until I escaped the darkness and could again see the light carried by my Divemaster. My best friend followed a moment later and together, we exited the cave and ascended slowly to the surface.

So what happened in the cave that day? The answer is a quick lesson in physics.

As you go deeper underwater, air pressure increases and volume decreases. As a diver, you have to continually adjust the air in your vest to maintain neutral buoyancy. Too much air and you'll float to the surface, too little air and you'll sink to the bottom.

It turns out that my best friend had lost buoyancy at the bottom of the cave and had started to sink. Rather than adding air to his vest to float up a bit, he instinctively kicked his fins a few times to swim up, in the process, stirring up all the silt and sediment on the bottom of the cave floor. The water became so clouded that visibility went from perfect to zero in a matter of seconds. It never would have cleared in time for us to find our way out.

That rope saved me. But it wasn't my rope. I didn't bring it. It was left there long ago, anchored to the cave walls by those who had come here before me. They left it for me and others who might get lost and need a way out.

The Christian faith is not something that we just believe, but it is something that we receive. The faith has been handed down, one generation to the next, for over two millennium. We don't get to pick and choose what we want to believe and not believe. Christianity is not an a la carte menu of theological treats or spiritual snacks. It's a faith tradition passed down to us. It's a guide rope anchored on the walls of a dark cave to guide us when we lose our way.

Wherever you go, whatever you choose to do, stay rooted in the faith. Be connected to a faith family somewhere. You may not always have your parents, your college group, or your childhood friends to remind you and challenge you to seek the Lord. Find a community of people to live alongside as you walk out the purposes of God. We often hear about those who lose their faith in adulthood, but long before there is a loss of faith, there is a loss of identity. We forget who we are and whose we are. The best way that you can honor those who have invested in you – your parents, pastors, friends, and mentors – is to stay rooted and keep growing.

As you go through life, there will be moments where you will find yourself alone in the dark, disoriented, and wondering, "what am I going to do?"

The friends that were with you are suddenly out of sight. The light illuminating the way has diminished.

In those moments, keep the faith. Find the rope. Keep reaching and grasping, reaching and grasping for Jesus until you find Him again. He'll lead you out of the darkness and into the light.

From one generation to the next, the Christian faith has been passed on to be our anchor.

The journey ahead of you may feel uncertain. The truth is it always is. Hold the rope.

The Blessing

So like Aaron spoke to the Israelites all those years ago, let me speak these timeless words to you today. To offer you a blessing for your journey.

The Lord bless you and keep you,
The Lord make his face to shine upon you

And be gracious to you.
The Lord lift up his countenance upon you,
And give you peace.
In the name of the Father and the Son and the Holy Spirit.
Amen.

Let's *Connect.*

Thank you for picking up this book! Continue the journey with Jim at jcmckenzie.com, where you can:

✦ Shop merchandise and apparel from each of the chapters.

✦ Download a free question guide for personal reflection or group discussions.

✦ Subscribe to Jim's newsletter.

I can't wait to connect with you. / *Jim McKenzie*

www.jcmckenzie.com

BOOK INSPIRED
Merchandise

DID YOU FIND YOURSELF SAYING, *"I'D WEAR THAT ON A SHIRT!"* AS YOU READ THIS BOOK? WELL, YOU ACTUALLY CAN! VISIT MY MERCH STORE, AND TAKE YOUR PICK FROM BOOK INSPIRED SHIRTS, BAGS AND MUGS.

Find these *and more* at www.jcmckenzie.com

Acknowledgements

This book is the fulfillment of a dream that God first seeded in my heart with a prophetic prayer by Pastor Perry Comas in November 2000. Thank you for that affirming word, Perry. It gave me the confidence to believe it was possible. A special thanks to Janis Owens and Pastor Svend Wilbekin for their encouragement to start writing and keep writing in those early years.

A big shout-out to Todd Carstenn, my high school English teacher. Behind my fears and insecurities about writing (see Chapter 6), I was listening and learning. You challenged me to put forth the same effort in writing as I did in my other passions and showed me the power of our words. You taught me to use the sandwich method to write meaty paragraphs. And short sentences for emphasis. The Carstenn Dagger is still my most cherished prize in writing.

I'm thankful to all the students, staff, and leaders of The Rock School. I have garnered so much from my time with you over the past 20+ years. If there is any useful wisdom in this book, I learned it in my work at TRS. You journeyed with me in a pursuit to faithfully follow Jesus and that makes each of you a co-author of this book. I ain't lion, when I say you rock!

A heartfelt thanks to Arica Heise, my colleague and dear friend. You provided thoughtful and encouraging feedback on my writing and speaking through the years. I could hear your lavish praise in my head as I was writing each chapter.

I am indebted to Ruth Buchanan, my writing coach, who helped me to get this book out of my head and on to its pages. Your coaching sessions were always the perfect blend of help and hope. I thought I only needed accountability to get this book done on time, but I learned so much from your editorial feedback. I now know to how to write chapter hooks and to track changes in Microsoft Word. And to stop double-spacing after periods.

The ideas I share in this book are the result of many wonderful friendships formed over the past ten years. I was privileged to cross paths with so many amazing folks in Christian ministries and schools, whose life and work inspires me daily. You broadened my vision of the Christian faith and our place in God's good creation. Thank you, Dan Beerens, for being my connection to nearly every one of these people.

I am grateful to my beta readers who provided feedback on early drafts of the book: Kristin, Amber, Cisco, JR, Sadie, Allison, Rachel, and DeAnna. Your encouragement instilled confidence and your notes made the final draft so much better.

A big thanks to Nona Jones and Tom Dean for their guidance. Thank you to the publishing team at Genesis Publishing House. Your assistance was instrumental in helping this first-time author through the publishing process. Thank you, Sally McConn, for helping me launch this book into the world and for designing the coolest merch store ever!

I dedicated this book to my five children, Colby, Casey, Cooper, Carter, and Darcy. When I started writing it, I told myself that even if it was never published and no one read it, that it was worth the effort to be able to share it with my children. Kids, thanks for bringing so much joy to my life and for being so supportive of this book project. Even all those Sunday afternoons that I was at Starbucks writing instead of home with you.

Most of all, I'm thankful to my best friend and biggest fan, my wife, Hannah. She waited patiently for twenty years for me to write a book. She never pressed me about writing and when I began this project, she gave me the time and space needed to complete it. Thank you for letting me chase these God-dreams, even when they seem crazy. I love you, babe!

To the One True Guide, Jesus, thank you for your enduring love and leadership in my life.

Jim McKenzie has worked in K-12 education for 25+ years, including more than 20 years in leadership at a Christian school. He holds an M.Ed. from the University of Florida. Jim and his wife, Hannah, have five children and live in Gainesville, Florida. When he's not writing, speaking, or attending school events, Jim enjoys playing pickleball with friends.

Learn more at www.jcmckenzie.com.